A
GENTLEMAN
ABROAD

OTHER GENTLEMANNERS™ BOOKS

A GENTLEMAN ABROAD

A Concise Guide to Traveling
with Confidence and Courtesy

JOHN BRIDGES
AND
BRYAN CURTIS

Published by
THOMAS NELSON™
Since 1798

www.thomasnelson.com

Published in Nashville, Tennessee, by Thomas Nelson, Inc.

Thomas Nelson, Inc., titles may be purchased in bulk for
educational, business, fundraising, or sales promotional use. For
information, please e-mail SpecialMarkets@ThomasNelson.com.

Library of Congress Cataloging-in-Publication Data

Bridges, John, 1950–
     A gentleman abroad : a concise guide to traveling with
confidence and courtesy / John Bridges and Bryan Curtis.
         p. cm.
     ISBN-13: 978-1-4016-0311-3 (hardcover)
     ISBN-10: 1-4016-0311-4 (hardcover)
     ISBN-13: 978-1-4016-0310-6 (leather)
     ISBN-10: 1-4016-0310-6 (leather)
     1. Travel etiquette. 2. Etiquette for men. I. Curtis,
Bryan, 1960– II. Title.
BJ2137.B75 2007
910.2'02—dc22

                                        2006100642

Printed in the United States of America

07 08 09 10 11 — 5 4 3 2 1

Contents

Introduction

Whenever a gentleman travels abroad, he has a dream in mind. Even if he travels frequently on business or for pleasure, he always fantasizes about a trip that will be everything he wishes it to be.

He holds his breath in hopes of seeing all the sites he has read about. He hopes for afternoons at small cafés and long, lingering evenings at fine restaurants. He imagines himself strolling through sidewalk markets, bargaining for a special keepsake, and later pointing it out to his friends as he shares the story of how he picked it up in Paris or Madrid or Sydney.

He envisions himself at the opera at the Grand Arena in Verona, in the bleachers for the World Cup Finals, in the stalls for a play in London's West End, or on a streetside in Bangkok, hearing music such as he has never heard before.

For the gentleman who still envisions travel as a wondrous experience, an escape from the workaday world, this book opens all those doors. What's more, it reminds every gentleman that there are universal laws of courtesy. Although other people may crowd in front of the line, or snap photos or run video cameras in art museums, a gentleman resists all temptations to act like an "ugly American." He waits his turn and takes his time. He turns off his camcorder when he is instructed to do so. He enjoys his experience, luxuriantly. He does not hurry. He is calm.

Travel restrictions change, but the urge to travel remains the same. Whenever a gentleman travels abroad—by air, by ship, by train, or by car—he is fulfilling a dream. He is making memories. He does his best to make sure they are good memories—or at least unique, irreplaceable ones—so he can cherish them for a lifetime to come.

A Note on the Foreign Phrases

For each city where the official language is not English, we have included several gentlemanly phrases. These are in no way representative of all the words and phrases a gentleman might attempt to master before visiting these locales. A gentleman would be wise to purchase a foreign language dictionary as well as an audio program in order to learn the proper pronunciation of the words and phrases he will need.

For the English-speaking destinations, we have included a sampling of words and phrases that differ from their American counterparts. An informed gentleman knows that even though English may be spoken in a foreign country, some of the usage may be unfamiliar.

78 Things Every Gentleman Who Travels Abroad Should Know

A gentleman travels to other countries in order to experience different cultures, taste new foods, and expose himself to new experiences.

—————

A gentleman does not assume that his own culture is superior to that of every other nation on the globe.

—————

A gentleman understands that, in every language, "please" and "thank you" are the most important words he can learn. He uses them frequently, knowing that the more often he uses them, the closer he will come to sounding like a native.

—————

A gentleman knows that simply speaking more loudly will not help a non-English-speaking person understand him one bit more clearly.

—————

If a gentleman does not speak the language of the country in which he is traveling, he does not pretend otherwise. He is not afraid to say to the clerk in any shop, the server in any restaurant, or the police officer on any street corner, "Excuse me. Do you speak English?"

———

A gentleman is never ashamed to ask, "Would you mind saying that again, a little more slowly, please?"

———

A gentleman resists using profanity at all times, but he is especially careful to do so in foreign countries, where cursing may be considered a dire affront or even a religious abomination.

———

A gentleman does not assume that, simply because he does not understand the language of the country he is visiting, the people of that country do not understand English. Because he is a gentleman, he is careful of what he says at all times.

———

A gentleman may wish to travel with an organized tour group, with a small group of friends or family, or on his own. At the end of any trip, he hopes to have made new friends—and kept his old ones.

———

A gentleman is not expected to salute the flag of a foreign country. He salutes the flag of his own country, however, on all ceremonial occasions.

———

A gentleman is not expected to bow or kneel in homage to a foreign dignitary or to the leader of a religion to which the gentleman is not an adherent.

———

A gentleman maintains a valid passport at all times.

———

A gentleman makes his travel arrangements, including his flight and hotel reservations, well ahead of time—not merely to save money but also to make sure he will be able to travel when he wishes and stay in accommodations that are up to his standards.

———

If a gentleman abhors crowded airports and masses of jet-lagged tourists, he travels off-season.

———

A gentleman keeps track of the time zone he is in.

———

If a gentleman is traveling with a tour group, or with a group of friends or family members, he does his best to be on time for scheduled events, especially for any scheduled departures.

———

If a gentleman is traveling by air, he takes care not to overindulge when the cocktail cart comes down the aisle. He may think that another glass of wine, or another shot of whiskey, will help him doze off and lessen the likelihood of jet lag. Instead, it may only make his arrival even more agonizing.

———

A gentleman knows that in most foreign countries he will be expected to pay for his program at the theatre. He also knows that he will be expected to tip the usher who helps him to his seat.

A gentleman does not drop trash on the street, either in his home country or in the countries of others.

———

If a gentleman is in a city or country where smoking is prohibited in public places, he does not light up.

———

If a nonsmoking gentleman is in a city or country where smoking is universally permitted, he does not complain. Instead, he does his best to get away from the smoke.

———

A gentleman treats the clerks in stores, the servers in restaurants, and the staff at his hotel with simple dignity and respect.

———

A gentleman remembers that, if he makes any purchase while he is abroad, he will have to pay the tax for it and figure out some way to get it home.

———

Unless a gentleman is very familiar with the city he is visiting, he does not roam the streets alone at night.

———

If a gentleman feels the urge to take a late-night stroll, he asks the front desk staff at his hotel which streets are the safest for his walk.

———

If a gentleman plans to shop for clothes while he is abroad, he remembers that clothing sizes in foreign countries are almost invariably different from the ones he is used to in the United States.

———

When packing for a trip abroad, a gentleman makes sure to carry underwear that is easy to wash and, more important, easy to dry. He may discover that boxer shorts travel better than heavy cotton briefs.

———

A gentleman takes special care to safeguard his wallet and his other valuables while traveling abroad. Although he may consider it adverse to his personal taste, he would be wise to carry them in a zippered pouch, securely fastened to his belt.

———

When making his way through even the most crowded streets or alleyways, a gentleman does not push or shove.

———

If a gentleman is offered a dish with which he is not familiar, and especially if it looks a trifle threatening to him, he is perfectly correct in saying, "Well, this certainly looks interesting. Would you mind telling me what it is?"

———

When a gentleman visits any foreign city— especially if it is a large city—he makes sure to carry a map or guidebook with him at all times.

———

A gentleman does not attempt to make jokes about the possibility of terrorist attacks, bomb threats, or the likelihood of natural disasters. Such jokes are never amusing.

———

Although he may not be fluent in a foreign language, a gentleman always learns a few all-important words and phrases, such as "Excuse me, please," "How much does this cost?" and "Which way to the restroom?"

———

Just as he would do in his own country, a gentleman does not use his cell phone in a house of worship, in an art museum, or during a performance in a theatre.

———

In most cases, a gentleman removes his hat or cap when entering a house of worship. In some cultures, however, he will be expected to cover his head. In such instances, he may even be offered an appropriate head covering. If he is offered such, he puts it on and wears it until he leaves the building.

———

If a gentleman, while visiting a house of worship, notices signage prohibiting videotaping or the taking of photographs, he puts his camera and his camcorder away. He can rest assured that picture postcards and souvenir booklets will most likely be available in a convenient gift shop.

———

A gentleman makes it a point to learn how to greet and be introduced to people in the country he is visiting. In Japan, for instance, he will remember to bow slightly from the waist when being introduced to a man or to a woman.

———

If a gentleman has been warned not to drink the water, he does not drink it.

———

When planning a trip abroad, a gentleman checks with his doctor or his travel agent to make sure he receives all necessary inoculations well ahead of his departure date.

———

If a gentleman takes prescription medicines, he makes sure to take along an ample supply, along with replacement prescriptions.

———

If a gentleman wears hearing aids, he makes sure to carry along an ample supply of batteries.

———

If a gentleman wears eyeglasses, he carries along an extra pair, as well as a copy of his eyeglasses prescription.

———

In a museum, a gentleman does not step in front of others who are attempting to enjoy the artwork.

———

If a gentleman finds himself in a situation where he finds he must pass between a fellow museum-goer and a painting or sculpture, he says, "Excuse me," even if he is not sure his fellow museum-goer understands English.

———

A gentleman knows that in some cultures it is not considered correct for him to shake hands with women, or even to speak with them.

———

Although back in his home country a gentleman may not be prone to stand patiently in line, he does so in foreign countries—particularly in England, where he will be expected to "queue up" to enter the subway, to purchase a ticket to the theatre, or even to enter the theatre itself.

———

Even if he has packed only his most casual traveling clothes, a gentleman does his best to dress in a dignified and respectful manner when visiting a house of worship of any religion, in any country.

———

Even when he is traveling in a hot climate, a gentleman dresses as respectably as possible. He does not walk bare-chested through the public streets. Even if he is wearing a T-shirt, he makes sure it is a clean T-shirt.

———

A gentleman has his hair cut the day before he departs on his visit to a foreign country.

———

A gentleman never expects the people of a foreign country to accept American dollars simply because that is the only cash he has on hand.

———

A gentleman does not give money to vagrants, even if they are small children.

———

If a gentleman discovers that his credit cards or his traveler's checks are missing, he contacts the issuer of the card or the checks immediately.

———

Even if a gentleman is confident he has identified the thief who has pilfered his property, he does not confront the alleged thief directly. Instead, he seeks the assistance of a police officer.

———

If a gentleman hopes to attend a popular event, such as an important music festival, a performance of a long-running play, or a major sports competition, he arranges for his tickets before he leaves home, calling upon the assistance of a travel agent, if necessary.

———

If a gentleman is uncertain about making his own reservations, especially in a city where English is not commonly spoken, he does not hesitate to call a travel agent.

———

Even if his travel plans do not include extended hiking excursions, a gentleman carries a sturdy pair of walking shoes with him whenever he goes abroad.

———

A gentleman does not attempt to carry home foodstuffs or other items that will cause delays or that may even be taken away from him at customs.

———

When a gentleman is making a purchase in a store or paying his tab in a restaurant, and is not confident in his understanding of the local currency, he may have no alternative except to ask for assistance from the clerk or the server in the restaurant. He knows that, with their help, he is probably more likely to receive the correct change than if he attempts to fumble with the coins and paper bills himself.

———

When he is in unfamiliar surroundings, a gentleman does his best to remain alert to street signs and other landmarks.

———

A gentleman does not take photographs in art museums or during performances in a theatre.

———

If a gentleman is attending a performance at an open-air arena or coliseum, he may take as many photographs as he pleases.

———

Before a gentleman travels to any foreign country, he does his best to read up on that country's history and customs.

———

If a gentleman expects to visit the beach while he is abroad, he makes sure to pack his preferred brand of sunscreen.

———

A gentleman knows that he will be expected to tip any attendant who offers him assistance at the beach.

———

A gentleman does not wear shorts while visiting the Vatican.

———

A gentleman knows that in many foreign countries minimal beach attire is a simple fact of life. If he is made uncomfortable by, or disapproves of, such display, he reconsiders visiting the beach.

———

If a gentleman is given the privilege of a private visit to a royal residence, an embassy, or some other site that is not usually open to the general public, he dresses appropriately. A suit and tie will probably be his best option.

———

A gentleman does his best to decrease the disorientation of jet lag. He takes a nap—even if it is a short one—immediately upon reaching his hotel room.

———

If a gentleman is carrying home valuable purchases (items other than inexpensive mementos such as postcards, guidebooks, and souvenir coffee mugs), he declares them openly, readily, and honestly to the customs agent.

———

If a gentleman has food allergies, he takes extra care when ordering his breakfast, lunch, or dinner, no matter what country he is traveling in.

———

Before departing for a trip to a foreign country, a gentleman visits a bank to make sure he has at least a limited supply of that country's currency in his pocket. A gentleman always looks ahead in order to take care of expenses that are sure to arise as soon as he arrives, even before he reaches his hotel.

———

If a gentleman plans to participate in an athletic activity such as golf or skiing when he is on a vacation, he checks about equipment rental in advance of his arrival.

———

While a gentleman may find it a romantic notion to ride a Vespa through the streets of Rome or run with the bulls in Pamplona, he takes a serious look at how equipped he really is to undertake those challenges before putting himself and others in physical danger.

———

Unless a gentleman considers himself an expert at bargaining, he does not haggle with street vendors. A gentleman understands, however, that in some cultures, particularly in the Middle East and the Far East, the buyer is expected to haggle with the vendor.

———

When crossing the border between countries, a gentleman always has his passport and other credentials close at hand. A gentleman keeps his passport ready at all times, no matter what.

———

A gentleman does not disparage the religious beliefs he encounters in any foreign country.

———

A gentleman does his best not to feel intimidated by cultures and customs that are different from his own.

———

When a gentleman asks for assistance, anywhere, in any country, he does so with a smile.

———

Amsterdam,
The Netherlands

Boats drift on the canals that wend their way through the city. Yes, this is one of Europe's most uninhibited cities, but it was also Rembrandt's hometown. The same slant of light that lit his paintings still lights up the late afternoon.

Distance from Other Cities

107 miles from Brussels

221 miles from London

357 miles from Berlin

3,645 miles from New York

4,114 miles from Chicago

5,563 miles from Los Angeles

Average Monthly Temperature

Month	Low	High
January	31	40
February	31	42
March	34	48
April	38	55
May	45	63
June	50	68

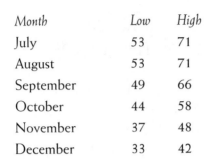

Month	Low	High
July	53	71
August	53	71
September	49	66
October	44	58
November	37	48
December	33	42

TIME DIFFERENCE

When it is 10:00 a.m. in Amsterdam . . .

it is 4:00 a.m. in New York

it is 3:00 a.m. in Chicago

it is 1:00 a.m. in Los Angeles

AMERICAN EMBASSY

The nearest office is located in The Hague.

Lange Voorhout 102

2514 EJ The Hague , Netherlands

Telephone: +31 70-310-2209

Fax: +31 70-361-4688

CURRENCY

Euro

DRIVING

A gentleman drives on the right side of the road.

Electricity

230 V   50 Hz

Tipping

Restaurants: As a service charge is included at most restaurants, a gentleman does not tip unless he feels exceptional service has warranted it.

Cabs: A gentleman leaves a tip of 10% of the fare.

Hotel assistance: 1 euro per bag

Gentlemanly Phrases

English	*Dutch*
Hello	Hallo
Good-bye	Tot ziens
Please	Alstublieft
Thank you	Dank u
You're welcome	Graag gedaan
Good morning	Goedemorgen
Good night	Goedenacht
Yes	Ja
No	Nee
Excuse me	Pardon
Pleased to meet you	Aangenaam
How are you?	Hoe gaat het met je?

English	Dutch
Fine, thanks	Goed, dank u wel
I don't understand	Ik begrijp het
English	Engels

TRADITIONAL TOAST

Proost

An informed gentleman is aware that Amsterdam is home to art museums that house the works of great masters such as Rembrandt. It is also the home of the notorious sex museum. If such establishments bother a gentleman, he avoids them.

ATHENS, GREECE

The cradle of democracy, ancient Athens was also the birthplace of great playwrights and legendary athletes. High above the city, the Parthenon, the most majestic monument in all of antiquity, still fills the soul with awe.

DISTANCE FROM OTHER CITIES
 188 miles from Thessaloniki
 349 miles from Istanbul
 654 miles from Rome
 4,927 miles from New York
 5,441 miles from Chicago
 6,902 miles from Los Angeles

AVERAGE MONTHLY TEMPERATURE

Month	Low	High
January	44	56
February	45	57
March	47	60
April	53	66
May	60	75
June	68	83
July	73	88

Month	Low	High
August	72	88
September	67	82
October	59	73
November	53	66
December	48	59

TIME DIFFERENCE

When it is 10:00 a.m. in Athens . . .

it is 3:00 a.m. in New York

it is 2:00 a.m. in Chicago

it is midnight in Los Angeles

AMERICAN EMBASSY

91 Vassilisis Sophia Avenue

Athens, 10160, Greece

Telephone: +30 210-721-2951

CURRENCY

Euro

DRIVING

A gentleman drives on the right side of the road.

ELECTRICITY

220 V   50 Hz

Tipping

Restaurants: A service charge will be included, but it is customary for a gentleman to leave an additional 5%–10% of the bill.

Cabs: A gentleman leaves a tip by rounding up the fare to the nearest euro.

Hotel assistance: 1 euro per bag

Gentlemanly Phrases

English	Greek
Hello	Yassou
Good-bye	Andio
Please	Parakalo
Thank you	Efcharisto
You're welcome	Parakalo
Good morning	Kalimera
Good night	Kalimichta
Yes	Nai
No	Ochi
Excuse me	Signomi
How are you?	Ti kanete?
I don't understand	Then katalaveno
English	Anglika

Traditional Toast
Eis Igian

———

An informed gentleman knows ouzo is a
strong drink and is careful when enjoying it as
an appetizer prior to a meal, or as an after-
dinner drink.

AUCKLAND, NEW ZEALAND

This is a city like no other, a place surrounded by kiwi trees and the cones of volcanoes—a place where you can hear the uniquely musical lilt of the Maori language. Faraway though it may be, it has stolen the hearts of explorers and adventurers, time and time again. That's why it is known as the City of 100 Lovers.

DISTANCE FROM OTHER CITIES
306 miles from Wellington
444 miles from Christchurch
1,340 miles from Sydney
6,257 miles from Los Angeles
8,203 miles from Chicago
8,831 miles from New York

AVERAGE MONTHLY TEMPERATURE

Month	Low	High
January	62	73
February	62	73
March	60	71
April	56	66

Month	Low	High
May	52	62
June	49	58
July	47	56
August	48	58
September	50	60
October	52	62
November	55	66
December	58	69

TIME DIFFERENCE

When it is 10:00 a.m. in Auckland . . .

it is 6:00 p.m. the previous day in New York

it is 5:00 p.m. the previous day in Chicago

it is 3:00 p.m. the previous day in Los Angeles

AMERICAN EMBASSY

The American embassy in New Zealand is located in Wellington.

29 Fitzherbert Terrace

Thorndon, Wellington, New Zealand

Telephone: +64 4-462-6000

Fax: +64 4-499-0490

CURRENCY

New Zealand dollar

DRIVING

A gentleman drives on the left side of the road.

ELECTRICITY

230 V　　　50 Hz

TIPPING

Tipping in New Zealand is not expected.
However, if a gentleman has received
exceptional service, he may wish to tip his server
in a restaurant or his driver 10% of the bill.

NEW ZEALAND PHRASES

Note: English is spoken here.

New Zealand	American
Biscuit	Cookie
Bloke	Man
Chemist	Pharmacy
Good on ya, mate	Congratulations
Kiwi	New Zealander
Lift	Elevator
Loo	Bathroom
Knickers	Underwear

New Zealand	American
Serviette	Napkin used to wipe hands and mouth at tea
Take-aways	Food to go

TRADITIONAL TOAST

Kia ora

———

An informed gentleman is especially careful to obey the speed limit when he ventures out of Auckland by car. He is also careful to keep his eye on the road instead of the beautiful scenery. The New Zealand countryside is notoriously hilly and mountainous, and the roads can be treacherous unless speeds are kept low and attention is paid to the road.

Big Days

A gentleman will be well-advised to remember that every country, every nation, and every city rejoices in its own annual celebrations. He schedules his travel accordingly.

He may wish to be part of the celebration of St. Patrick's Day in Dublin, and all the festivity that surrounds it. But he will also be well forewarned that a "Bank Holiday" in London means a day when almost all businesses are shut down.

He does not assume, of course, that foreign countries acknowledge holidays—such as the Fourth of July or Thanksgiving Day—that are essentially U.S. in origin. He may be bemused, however, to learn that other countries acknowledge Christmas and New Year's in other ways. In the U.K., Boxing Day, the day after Christmas (and the day on which masters traditionally gave presents to their servants) is almost as important a holiday as Christmas Day itself. It is a day when businesses are generally closed and families and friends gather for quiet, post-Christmas celebrations.

Other celebrations, however, will be unlike anything a gentleman from the United States has ever experienced before. For example, the traditional Running of the Bulls, in the midst of summer in Pamplona, Spain, is a grandiose yet chaotic spectacle. A gentleman would never plan to be there, unless he wanted to risk being battered in the streets.

Bangkok, Thailand

Taxis, buses, and the subway are readily available, of course, but it seems much more exotic to be whisked from ancient palaces to ancient temples in an open-air, three-wheeled *tuk-tuk*. In a city where neighbors regularly call one another "brother" and "sister," the welcome will be warm—but be prepared to bargain.

Distance from Other Cities
891 miles from Singapore
1,072 miles from Hong Kong
1,787 miles from Shanghai
7,568 miles from Chicago
8,273 miles from Los Angeles
8,664 miles from New York

Average Monthly Temperature

Month	Low	High
January	71	89
February	75	90
March	78	92
April	80	94
May	80	92

Month	Low	High
June	80	91
July	78	90
August	78	90
September	77	89
October	77	89
November	74	88
December	70	87

TIME DIFFERENCE

When it is 10:00 a.m. in Bangkok . . .

it is 11:00 p.m. the previous day in New York

it is 10:00 p.m. the previous day in Chicago

it is 8:00 p.m. the previous day in Los Angeles

AMERICAN EMBASSY

95 Wireless Road,
Bangkok 10330, Thailand
Telephone: +66 2-205-4000

CURRENCY

Baht

DRIVING

A gentleman drives on the left side of the road.

ELECTRICITY

220 V   50 Hz

TIPPING

Restaurants: A gentleman leaves a tip of 10% of the bill, if no service charge has been added.

Cabs: A gentleman leaves a tip by rounding up the fare to the nearest baht.

Hotel assistance: 20 baht per bag

GENTLEMANLY PHRASES

English	Thai
Hello	Sawatdi
Good-bye	Lagon
Please	Karuna
Thank you	Khap khun
You're welcome	Mai pen rai
Good morning	Sawatdi torn chao
Good night	Ra-tree sawat
Yes	Chai
No	Mai chai
Excuse me	Khow thoht
How are you?	Sabai dee rue?

English	Thai
English	*Thai*
I don't understand	Mai khao jai
English	Angknit

TRADITIONAL TOAST
Sawasdi

An informed gentleman knows that Thailand is a Buddhist country where images of Buddha are held sacred. A foreign visitor risks imprisonment should he fail to treat these images with due respect and reverence.

Beijing, China

The Great Wall takes the breath away. The Temple of Heaven rises upward toward the skies, and it is only right to be astounded at the glories of a city that is a thousand years old. Beijing is every bit as busy as it appears to be in TV news footage, but its reverence for tradition is timeless.

Distance from Other Cities

67 miles from Tianjin

668 miles from Shanghai

1,225 miles from Hong Kong

6,257 miles from Los Angeles

6,596 miles from Chicago

6,883 miles from New York

Average Monthly Temperature

Month	Low	High
January	19	34
February	19	39
March	30	52
April	45	67
May	55	79

Month	Low	High
June	64	86
July	70	87
August	68	85
September	57	78
October	45	66
November	31	30
December	19	37

TIME DIFFERENCE

When it is 10:00 a.m. in Beijing . . .

it is 10:00 p.m. the previous day in New York

it is 9:00 p.m. the previous day in Chicago

it is 7:00 p.m. the previous day in Los Angeles

AMERICAN EMBASSY

Xiu Shui Bei Jie 3, 100600
Beijing, China
Telephone: +86 10-6532-3831

CURRENCY

RMB/yuan

Driving

A gentleman drives on the right side of the road.

Electricity

220 V   50 Hz

Tipping

Restaurants: If no service charge has been added, the addition of a tip is left to a gentleman's discretion.

Cabs: No tip is necessary.

Hotel assistance: 5 yuan per bag

Gentlemanly Phrases

English	Chinese
Hello	Ninhao
Good-bye	Zaijian
Please	Qing
Thank you	Xiexie
You're welcome	Bu xie
Good morning	Nin zao
Good night	Wan an
Yes	Shi
No	Bu
Excuse me	Duibuqi

English	Chinese
How are you?	Ni hao ma?
Fine, thanks	Hao xiexie
I don't understand	Wo bu dong
English	Yingwen

TRADITIONAL TOAST
Wen lei

———

An informed gentleman knows that travel in China can be strenuous. Tours often involve walking long distances and up steep hills. Knowing your physical limitations and not trying to do more than is possible will make the difference between a good trip and a miserable one.

BERLIN, GERMANY

Always at the cutting edge of the avant-garde,
Berlin boasts a stunning wealth of contemporary
architecture and rich troves of modern art. Very
little of the Berlin Wall remains, but it will do
the heart good to pause for a few minutes and
remember the day it came down.

DISTANCE FROM OTHER CITIES
262 miles from Frankfurt

279 miles from Bonn

312 miles from Munich

3,969 miles from New York

4,408 miles from Chicago

5,792 miles from Los Angeles

AVERAGE MONTHLY TEMPERATURE

Month	Low	High
January	26	33
February	28	38
March	32	46
April	39	55
May	46	65
June	52	71

Month	Low	High
July	55	73
August	54	73
September	48	65
October	42	55
November	35	44
December	30	37

TIME DIFFERENCE

When it is 10:00 a.m. in Berlin . . .

it is 4:00 a.m. in New York

it is 3:00 a.m. in Chicago

it is 1:00 a.m. in Los Angeles

AMERICAN EMBASSY

Neustädtische Kirchstr. 4-5

10117 Berlin

Federal Republic of Germany

Telephone: +49 30-2385-174

CURRENCY

Euro

DRIVING

A gentleman drives on the right side of the road.

Electricity
230 V   50 Hz

Tipping

Restaurants: A gentleman adds 5%–10% of the bill in addition to the service charge already included

Cabs: Tipping is not traditional, but if a gentleman has received exceptional service, he may wish to tip 5%–10% of his fare.

Hotel assistance: 1 euro per bag

Gentlemanly Phrases

English	*German*
Hello	Guten Tag
Good-bye	Auf Wiedersehen
Please	Bitte
Thank you	Danke
You're welcome	Bitte schön
Good morning	Guten Morgen
Good night	Gute Nacht
Yes	Ja
No	Nein
Excuse me	Entschuldigen Sie
Pleased to meet you	Sie kennenzulernen

English	German
How are you?	Wie geht es Ihnen?
Fine, thanks	Gut, danke
I don't understand	Ich verstehe nicht
English	Englisch

TRADITIONAL TOAST

Prosit

An informed gentleman knows that Germans traditionally enjoy their biggest meal of the day at noon and eat a lighter meal in the evening hours.

In the Bag

At least for most gentlemen, the days are gone when a trip abroad required steamer trunks full of toiletries, custom-tailored suits, and handmade shoes. The well-traveled man travels with as few bags as possible, editing his wardrobe as efficiently as possible.

When planning his trip, a gentleman makes sure to check out the likely weather conditions in the cities he will be visiting. Then he packs accordingly. If he is headed to Spain in the height of summer, he does not lug along an overcoat. If he is headed to London in October, however, he will be wise to take along a raincoat and a cotton sweater as well.

If a gentleman knows he will be spending a night at the opera, the theatre, or a concert hall—and unless his seats are in the top balcony—he packs a sports coat and a pair of long trousers. Cargo shorts and T-shirts are fine for strolling through sidewalk markets and touring the ruins of Athens and Rome; but a gentleman will dress in a somewhat more dignified manner when dining in a fine restaurant or visiting one of the world's great houses of worship.

Before he leaves home, a gentleman will be wise to equip himself with a pair of comfortable shoes that will be appropriate for almost any occasion. (A simple, sturdy pair of black walking shoes will see him through a night at the opera, an evening at a four-star restaurant, or an afternoon in the bleachers at the World Cup Finals.)

A gentleman selects luggage that is durable and easy to handle. A lightweight bag, of durable fabric and equipped with rollers, is a virtual necessity for a trip of almost any length. He makes sure it is a bag that can be easily opened for inspection.

In every case, if a gentleman plans to carry his suitcase on the airplane, on a train, or on a bus, he makes sure it will fit in the overhead compartments. If he learns that air-travel regulations are likely to severely restrict what he may carry on the plane, he will be well-advised to check his bag. Upon arrival at his destination, he may find the delay at baggage claim tedious, but he considers it a small inconvenience, compared to the possibility of arriving with no baggage at all, simply because the contents of his suitcase violated air-travel regulations.

Bogotá, Colombia

Known as one of the world's best-mannered and best-read cities, Bogotá may challenge a gentleman to be on his best behavior. An entire museum is filled with artifacts crafted of gold—nothing else in the world can match such wonders.

DISTANCE FROM OTHER CITIES

153 miles from Medellín
191 miles from Cali
633 miles from Caracas
2,485 miles from New York
2,696 miles from Chicago
3,487 miles from Los Angeles

AVERAGE MONTHLY TEMPERATURE

Month	Low	High
January	41	67
February	43	67
March	45	67
April	46	64
May	47	66
June	46	64
July	45	64

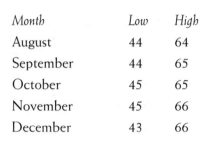

Month	Low	High
August	44	64
September	44	65
October	45	65
November	45	66
December	43	66

TIME DIFFERENCE

When it is 10:00 a.m. in Bogotá . . .

it is 11:00 a.m. in New York

it is 10:00 a.m. in Chicago

it is 8:00 a.m. in Los Angeles

AMERICAN EMBASSY

Carrera 45 # 22D-45

Bogotá, D.C., Colombia

Telephone: +57 1-315-0811

CURRENCY

Colombian peso

DRIVING

A gentleman drives on the right side of the road.

ELECTRICITY

110 V   60 Hz

Tipping

Restaurants: A gentleman adds 10% to his total if a service charge hasn't been added to his bill.

Cabs: A gentleman does not need to leave a tip unless the driver assists with baggage.

Hotel assistance: 2 Colombian pesos per bag

Gentlemanly Phrases

English	Spanish
Hello	Hola
Good-bye	Adiós
Please	Por favor
Thank you	Gracias
You're welcome	De nada
Good morning	Buenos días
Good night	Buenas noches
Yes	Sí
No	No
Excuse me	Con permiso
Pleased to meet you	Mucho gusto
How are you?	¿Cómo está usted?
Fine, thanks	Bien, gracias
I don't understand	No entiendo
English	Inglés

Traditional Toast
Salud

———

An informed gentleman knows that because Colombians are among the most polite and formal citizens in the world, a "please" and "thank you" should accompany every request and response to that request.

BOMBAY (MUMBAI), INDIA

The movies of "Bollywood" paint a colorful picture of modern-day India, but they scarcely match the real colors of Bombay, a city that jostles along, rich with the textures of exquisite silks and the sultry aroma of saffron.

DISTANCE FROM OTHER CITIES

721 miles from New Delhi
1,033 miles from Calcutta
2,676 miles from Hong Kong
7,801 miles from New York
8,061 miles from Chicago
8,710 miles from Los Angeles

AVERAGE MONTHLY TEMPERATURE

Month	Low	High
January	66	85
February	68	85
March	72	88
April	77	90
May	80	92
June	79	89
July	77	86

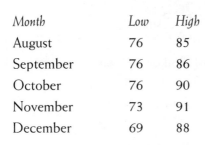

Month	Low	High
August	76	85
September	76	86
October	76	90
November	73	91
December	69	88

TIME DIFFERENCE

When it is 10:00 a.m. in Bombay . . .

it is 12:30 a.m. the previous day in New York

it is 11:30 p.m. the previous day in Chicago

it is 9:30 p.m. the previous day in Los Angeles

AMERICAN CONSULATE

Lincoln House

78 Bhulabhai Desai Road

Mumbai (Bombay) 400 026, India

Telephone: +22 2363-3611

Fax: +22 2363-0350

ELECTRICITY

240 V   50 Hz

CURRENCY

Rupee

DRIVING

A gentleman drives on the left side of the road.

TIPPING

Restaurants: A gentleman leaves 10%–15% of the bill as a tip, unless a service charge has been added.

Cabs: A gentleman leaves a tip of 10% of the fare.

Hotel assistance: 20 rupees per bag

GENTLEMANLY PHRASES

English	*Hindi*
Hello	Namaste
Good-bye	Alavidha
Please	Kripyaa
Thank you	Dhanyavaad
You're welcome	Aapakaa svaagat hai
Good morning	Shubha prabhaat
Good night	Shubha raatri
Yes	Ha
No	Nahi
Excuse me	Shamma kare

English	Hindi
Pleased to meet you	Aapse milkar khushii huyii
How are you?	Aap kaise hai?
Fine	Achchhey
I don't understand	Mai nahii samajta hu
English	Angrejii

TRADITIONAL TOAST

Aap ki sehat ue liye

An informed gentleman knows that when shopping in hectic, disorganized markets, like those of Bombay, bargaining is both acceptable and expected. If he is uncomfortable with haggling, he shops in more standard retail establishments.

Brussels, Belgium

A dozen Belgian lace handkerchiefs would make a perfect memento of your days in bustling Brussels. But don't forget that this is also the City of Beer. A hearty stein of lager in a beer hall provides the perfect break after sightseeing in the centuries-old guild halls in the filigreed town square.

Distance from Other Cities

26 miles from Antwerp

115 miles from Luxembourg

163 miles from Paris

3,660 miles from New York

4,145 miles from Chicago

5,620 miles from Los Angeles

Average Monthly Temperature

Month	Low	High
January	31	41
February	32	43
March	35	48
April	40	54
May	46	63

Month	Low	High
June	51	67
July	54	71
August	54	71
September	50	66
October	45	57
November	37	48
December	33	42

TIME DIFFERENCE

When it is 10:00 a.m. in Brussels . . .

it is 4:00 a.m. in New York

it is 3:00 a.m. in Chicago

it is 1:00 a.m. in Los Angeles

AMERICAN EMBASSY

27 Boulevard du Regent B-1000

Brussels, Belgium

Telephone: +32 2-513-3830

Fax: +32 2-502-1490

CURRENCY

Euro

DRIVING

A gentleman drives on the right side of the road.

ELECTRICITY

220 V   50 Hz

TIPPING

Restaurants: As a rule, restaurant checks in Brussels include a service fee. If a gentleman has received exceptional service, he may wish to leave an additional 5%–10%.

Cabs: A service charge is included with each cab fare. If a gentleman is especially satisfied with his experience, he could tip his driver an additional 5% of his fare or round up the nearest euro.

Hotel assistance: 1 euro per bag

GENTLEMANLY PHRASES

Note: Dutch is also an official language in Belgium. For common phrases in Dutch, please see page 19.

English	*French*
Hello	Bonjour
Good-bye	Au revoir
Please	S'il vous plaît
Thank you	Merci
You're welcome	De rien
Good morning	Bonjour

English	French
Good night	Bonne nuit
Yes	Oui
No	Non
Excuse me	Pardonnez-moi
Pleased to meet you	Enchanté
How are you?	Comment allez-vous?
Fine , thanks	Bien, merci
I don't understand	Je ne comprends pas
English	Anglais

TRADITIONAL TOAST
Geluch

An informed gentleman knows that most cultural attractions in Brussels are open on Sundays and closed on Mondays. He plans his activities accordingly.

Departing Glances

When leaving for a trip overseas, or a return trip back home, a gentleman arrives at the airport at least 90 minutes prior to his flight's scheduled departure time. (When he is departing for the trip home, from an overseas airport, he will be well-advised to arrive even two hours before his scheduled departure, since he will have to deal with customs, and, potentially, with additional inspections.)

He knows that, because he is traveling abroad, extra security scanning and surveillance may be required. A gentleman understands that all passengers will be undergoing the same scrutiny. He does not take it as a personal affront. Neither does he attempt to avoid going through the scrutiny process.

Upon arriving at the airport, prior to his departure, a gentleman immediately proceeds to the airline counter to check his bags (unless he is traveling with carry-on luggage only). He knows that, because he is traveling abroad, his luggage may be subjected to close examination. He submits to any inspections with all good grace. He does not slow down the process or harass the security personnel by shouting, "Hey, watch it! You're wrinkling my T-shirts."

From the moment he arrives at the airport, a gentleman keeps his passport, and any other necessary papers, at hand. (His travel agent or his airline's Web site will be able to tell him what papers he may need to carry with him.) Whenever he is asked to show his ID, he does so.

As his line moves closer to the security checkpoint, a gentleman removes his shoes, his belt, his hat or cap, and his coat, if he is wearing one. He places all these items, as well as his pocket change, his watch, his money clip, his cell phone, and his laptop (if he is carrying one), in the bins provided by the security personnel. He keeps his boarding pass with him, since the security officer will ask to see it when he passes through the metal detector.

If, for some reason, the security personnel must open the gentleman's carry-on bags for an additional safety check, or if they must subject him to an additional body screening, he does not grouse, "What's this about? Do I look like some kind of bomber?" Nor does he attempt to make jokes about terrorism and airplane disasters. Such remarks, if overheard by security personnel, who almost certainly will *not* find them amusing, may lead to his being removed from his flight.

When it is time for him to board his flight, a gentleman quietly takes his place in line and waits for his seat number to be called.

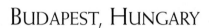

Budapest, Hungary

Once it was actually two cities, Buda and Pest. Although they're united as Hungary's glamorous capital city, a river still runs through them, that most magical river of all—the blue (or sometimes green) Danube.

Distance from Other Cities

89 miles from Miskolc

119 miles from Debrecen

135 miles from Vienna

4,358 miles from New York

4,820 miles from Chicago

6,221 miles from Los Angeles

Average Monthly Temperature

Month	Low	High
January	24	34
February	28	40
March	35	50
April	43	61
May	51	70
June	57	75
July	59	79

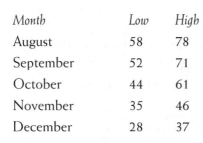

Month	Low	High
August	58	78
September	52	71
October	44	61
November	35	46
December	28	37

TIME DIFFERENCE

When it is 10:00 a.m. in Budapest . . .

it is 4:00 a.m. in New York

it is 3:00 a.m. in Chicago

it is 1:00 in Los Angeles

AMERICAN EMBASSY

Szabadság tér 12

H-1054 Budapest, Hungary

Telephone: +36 1-475-4400

CURRENCY

Forint

DRIVING

A gentleman drives on the right side of the road.

ELECTRICITY

230 V   50 Hz

TIPPING

Restaurants: A gentleman leaves a tip equal to 10%–15% of the bill.

Cabs: A gentleman leaves a tip of 10% of the fare.

Hotel: 200 forint per bag

GENTLEMANLY PHRASES

English	Hungarian
Hello	Jó napot
Good-bye	Viszontlátásra
Please	Kérem
Thank you	Köszönöm
You're welcome	Szívesen
Good morning	Jó reggelt
Good evening	Jó estét
Yes	Igen
No	Nem
Excuse me	Bocsánat
Pleased to meet you	Orvendek
I don't understand	Nem értem
English	Angolul

TRADITIONAL TOAST

Kedves egeszegere

An informed gentleman knows that Hungarians do not clink their beer glasses when making a toast. Such has been the tradition ever since the Austrians who led the 1848 revolution toasted the execution of Hungarian generals with beer. When modern-day Hungarians decline to clink their glasses, they demonstrate their continuing solidarity with those fallen generals.

BUENOS AIRES, ARGENTINA

In Buenos Aires, one of the world's most sensuous cities, it sometimes seems that pulses actually do throb to the languid rhythm of the tango. The European influences are rich and varied. The steaks, of course, are legendary.

DISTANCE FROM OTHER CITIES

398 miles from Córdoba

703 miles from Santiago

1,226 miles from Rio de Janeiro

5,305 miles from New York

5,604 miles from Chicago

6,126 miles from Los Angeles

AVERAGE MONTHLY TEMPERATURE

Month	Low	High
January	62	86
February	61	83
March	57	79
April	51	72
May	45	66
June	41	59
July	41	59

Month	Low	High
August	41	62
September	34	66
October	50	71
November	54	77
December	59	83

TIME DIFFERENCE

When it is 10:00 a.m. in Buenos Aires . . .

it is 9:00 a.m. in New York

it is 8:00 a.m. in Chicago

it is 6:00 a.m. in Los Angeles

AMERICAN EMBASSY

Av. Colombia 4300

(C1425GMN) Buenos Aires, Argentina

Telephone: +54 11-5777-4533

Fax: +54 11-5777-4240

CURRENCY

Argentinean peso

DRIVING

A gentleman drives on the right side of the road.

ELECTRICITY

220 V   50 Hz

TIPPING

Restaurants: A gentleman leaves a tip equal to 10% of the bill.

Cabs: Drivers traditionally round up cab fares to cover the tip. A gentleman should give an additional amount for exceptional service.

Hotel assistance: 2–3 pesos per bag

GENTLEMANLY PHRASES

English	Spanish
Hello	Hola
Good-bye	Adiós
Please	Por favor
Thank you	Gracias
You're welcome	De nada
Good morning	Buenos días
Good night	Buenas noches
Yes	Sí
No	No
Excuse me	Con permiso
Pleased to meet you	Mucho gusto
How are you?	¿Cómo está usted?

English	Spanish
Fine, thanks	Bien, gracias
I don't understand	No entiendo
English	Inglés

TRADITIONAL TOAST
Salud

———

An informed gentleman is aware that smoking is allowed virtually everywhere in Buenos Aires—movie theatres, public transportation, restaurants. He keeps this reality in mind if secondhand smoke is particularly bothersome to him.

CAIRO, EGYPT

It's difficult to say whether the pyramids are more impressive under the baking desert sun or in the blackness of the desert night, when they're lit up by the high drama of a sound-and-light show. The monumental pyramids continue to hold great mysteries and raise eternal questions, but the great Sphinx still declines to reveal the answers.

DISTANCE FROM OTHER CITIES

    5 miles from Giza

    113 miles from Alexandria

    313 miles from Luxor

    5,610 miles from New York

    6,136 miles from Chicago

    7,590 miles from Los Angeles

AVERAGE MONTHLY TEMPERATURE

Month	Low	High
January	49	65
February	50	68
March	54	73
April	59	82
May	64	89

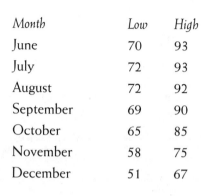

Month	Low	High
June	70	93
July	72	93
August	72	92
September	69	90
October	65	85
November	58	75
December	51	67

TIME DIFFERENCE

When it is 10:00 a.m. in Cairo . . .

it is 3:00 a.m. in New York

it is 2:00 a.m. in Chicago

it is midnight in Los Angeles

AMERICAN EMBASSY

8 Kamal El Din Salah St.
Garden City, Cairo, Egypt
Telephone: +20 2-797-3300

CURRENCY

Pound

DRIVING

A gentleman drives on the right side of the road.

ELECTRICITY

220 V   50 Hz

TIPPING

Restaurants: A gentleman leaves a tip of 10%–15% of the bill.

Cabs: A gentleman leaves a tip of 10%–15% of the fare.

Hotel assistance: 5 pounds per bag

GENTLEMANLY PHRASES

English	Egyptian Arabic
Hello	Ahlan wa sahlan
Good-bye	Salam
Please	Min fadlak
Thank you	Shukran
You're welcome	'Afuann
Good morning	Sahab el-kheir
Good night	Tisbah ala kheir
Yes	Aiwa
No	La
Excuse me	Assef
How are you?	Izayak?
Fine	Kiwayess
I don't understand	Mish fahiim
English	Englizee

TRADITIONAL TOAST
Fee sihetak

———

An informed gentleman knows the summer
heat in Egypt is like a furnace and packs
accordingly, bringing a wardrobe made of
breathable natural cotton fiber that fits loosely
and breathes easily.

The Help Desk

Most large hotels, and some of a more moderate size, offer the services of a concierge. The concierge is usually stationed at a desk in the hotel's main lobby and is available during regular working hours to assist hotel guests by answering questions of every sort. He or she can also frequently be of assistance in helping secure tickets to concerts, sporting events, art galleries, and the theatre. When it comes to selecting restaurants, a well-trained concierge is equipped with encyclopedic advice; when it comes to securing a hard-to-get reservation, the right concierge has all the right connections.

The concierge can also give advice as to the location of the nearest drugstore or the closest hospital. The concierge can provide clear, easy-to-follow directions or a map of the city. A good concierge offers dependable advice about public transit and about the safety of the neighborhood.

There is no direct charge for the concierge's services. (The expense of tickets secured by the concierge will be added to the guest's bill, usually with a service charge included.) If the concierge does provide a service, such as making a dinner reservation or securing a theatre ticket, a gentleman shows his gratitude with a tip. The size of the tip will vary according to the extent of the service. If the concierge has arranged for a dinner in a fine restaurant or for tickets to a long-running show, a gentleman will tip him with the equivalent of $20. For a less challenging service, such as watching over a gentleman's packages when he has just dashed in from a bout of shopping and must hurry along to his next appointment, a $5 tip is appropriate.

In hotels in the United States, a gentleman simply hands the concierge his tip, perhaps under the disguise of a handshake. In other countries, it is more traditional for a gentleman to enclose the tip in an envelope and place it on the concierge's desk, saying, "Thank you, Raul, for helping us with last night's reservation. Our dinner was lovely." or "Thank you, Ivan, for watching over my packages this afternoon."

If the gentleman has made no major demands on the concierge, but if he has asked for his assistance from time to time over the course of a couple of days at the hotel, he tips him $10 at checkout time. If a gentleman has stayed at the hotel more than two days and has asked for the concierge's assistance at all, he leaves $20, at least, in addition to any tips he might have left for specific services. If he has had no interaction with the concierge during his stay, he feels no need to leave any tip at all.

CAPE TOWN, SOUTH AFRICA

History tells of fearless explorers rounding the Cape in search of a route to the spice-rich East, but local legends tell of pirates holed up at the foot of Table Mountain or on the slopes of Devil's Peak. If a gentleman himself is feeling particularly fearless, he may opt for a close encounter (or at least as close an encounter as a diving cage allows) with the great white sharks in Shark Alley.

DISTANCE FROM OTHER CITIES

786 miles from Johannesburg

790 miles from Durban

815 miles from Pretoria

7,815 miles from New York

8,502 miles from Chicago

9,985 miles from Los Angeles

AVERAGE MONTHLY TEMPERATURE

Month	Low	High
January	63	77
February	63	78
March	60	76
April	56	72

Month	Low	High
May	52	67
June	48	64
July	47	62
August	48	63
September	51	65
October	54	69
November	58	72
December	61	75

TIME DIFFERENCE

When it is 10:00 a.m. in Cape Town . . .

it is 4:00 a.m. in New York

it is 3:00 a.m. in Chicago

it is 1:00 a.m. in Los Angeles

AMERICAN CONSULATE

2 Reddam Ave

Westlake 7945, South Africa

Mailing address:

PostNet Suite 50

Private Bag x26

Tokai 7966, South Africa

Tel: +27 21-702-7300

Fax: +27 21-702-7493

Currency

Rand

Driving

A gentleman drives on the left side of the road.

Electricity

220–230V   50 Hz

Tipping

Restaurants: A gentleman leaves 10% of the bill as a tip.

Cabs: A gentleman leaves a tip of 10% of the fare.

Hotel assistance: 5 rand per bag

Gentlemanly Phrases

English	*Afrikaans*
Hello	Hallo
Good-bye	Totsiens
Please	Asseblief
Thank you	Dankie
Good morning	Goeiemore
Good night	Goeienaang
Yes	Ja
No	Nee

English	Afrikaans
Excuse me	Verskoon my
Pleased to meet you	Aangename kennis
How are you?	Hoe gaan dit?
Fine, thanks	Goed, dankie
I don't understand	Ek verstaan jou nie
English	Engels

TRADITIONAL TOAST

Gesondheid

An informed gentleman knows that in South Africa eleven official languages are spoken. Luckily, English is commonly spoken throughout the country.

CARACAS, VENEZUELA

Caracas sits surrounded by the unspoiled
natural wonders of El Ávila National Park,
where butterflies and birds, unknown anywhere
else on the globe, flutter through the trees. At
least such natural wonders seem unspoiled for
the moment. A gentleman may wish to book his
visit soon, while they still flourish.

DISTANCE FROM OTHER CITIES
    77 miles from Valencia
    319 miles from Maracaibo
    422 miles from Scarborough, Tobago
    2,136 miles from New York
    2,507 miles from Chicago
    3,621 miles from Los Angeles

AVERAGE MONTHLY TEMPERATURE

Month	Low	High
January	71	83
February	71	83
March	72	83
April	74	84
May	76	86

Month	Low	High
June	76	87
July	75	86
August	76	88
September	76	89
October	76	88
November	75	87
December	73	85

TIME DIFFERENCE

When it is 10:00 a.m. in Caracas . . .

it is 10:00 a.m. in New York

it is 9:00 a.m. in Chicago

it is 7:00 a.m. in Los Angeles

AMERICAN EMBASSY

Calle F con Calle Suapure
Urb. Colinas de Valle Arriba
Caracas 1080, Venezuela
Telephone: +58 212-975-6411

CURRENCY

Bolivar

Driving

A gentleman drives on the right side of the road.

Electricity

120 V   60 Hz

Tipping

Restaurants: A service charge is generally added to each bill. A gentleman may wish to tip an additional amount if the service has been exceptional.

Cabs: A gentleman need not tip unless the driver assists with baggage.

Hotel assistance: 2 bolivares per bag

Gentlemanly Phrases

English	Spanish
Hello	Hola
Good-bye	Adiós
Please	Por favor
Thank you	Gracias
You're welcome	De nada
Good morning	Buenos días
Good night	Buenas noches
Yes	Sí
No	No

English	Spanish
Excuse me	Con permiso
Pleased to meet you	Mucho gusto
How are you?	¿Cómo está usted?
Fine, thanks	Bien, gracias
I don't understand	No entiendo
English	Inglés

TRADITIONAL TOAST
Salud

An informed gentleman knows that in Venezuela shorts are generally reserved for the beach areas and that gentlemen dress somewhat more conservatively in other areas of the city.

Casablanca, Morocco

You won't find Bogey and Bergman bidding each other a tearful good-bye at the airport, but you will be able to catch a cocktail at a bar that closely resembles Rick's Place. Modern-day Casablanca doesn't look much like the shadowy town in the movie, but in the Old Town, the air still holds a promise of adventure.

Distance from Other Cities

54 miles from Rabat
137 miles from Marrakesh
154 miles from Fez
3,604 miles from New York
4,257 miles from Chicago
5,962 miles from Los Angeles

Average Monthly Temperature

Month	Low	High
January	47	62
February	50	63
March	51	64
April	53	66
May	58	69

Month	Low	High
June	64	73
July	68	77
August	68	78
September	66	77
October	60	72
November	54	68
December	50	64

TIME DIFFERENCE

When it is 10:00 a.m. in Casablanca . . .

it is 6:00 a.m. in New York

it is 5:00 a.m. in Chicago

it is 4:00 a.m. in Los Angeles

AMERICAN EMBASSY

8 Boulevard Moulay Youssef

Casablanca, Morocco

Telephone: +212 22-43-05-78

Fax: +212 22-20-41-27

CURRENCY

Dirham

DRIVING

A gentleman drives on the right side of the road.

ELECTRICITY

127/220V   50 Hz

TIPPING

Restaurants: A gentleman leaves a tip of 10% of the bill, if a service charge hasn't been added.

Cabs: No tip is necessary, but a gentleman rounds up the fare to the nearest dirham.

Hotel assistance: 5 dirhams per bag

GENTLEMANLY PHRASES

English	Moroccan Arabic
Hello	Ssalamu lekum
Good-bye	Baslamma Besslama
Please	Afek
Thank you	Shoukran
You're welcome	Blajmeel
Good morning	S'bah l'khir
Good night	Tsba-alakhir
Yes	Iyeh
No	Laa
Excuse me	Smeh liya
Pleased to meet you	M'tsharafin
How are you?	La-bas?
Fine	Ana labas a

English	Moroccan Arabic
I don't understand	Ma ke nifhimsh
English	B'ingleezia

Traditional Toast
Saha wa afiab

An informed gentleman knows he may often find himself the center of unsolicited attention. In cities such as Casablanca, young boys hoping for money eagerly offer directions, hawk souvenirs, or offer to take a snapshot of a gentleman and his party. While he always remains courteous, a gentleman also remains wary of those offering such assistance.

DIRECTIONS INCLUDED

An Internet-savvy gentleman may think himself fully capable of planning a trip to any city in any country. The intricacies of booking his flights and his ground transportation, reserving his lodgings, securing his theatre tickets and access to all the major museums, and even setting up his own African safari may hold no fears for him.

However, if a gentleman is planning an especially complex trip, if he is not an expert Web surfer, if he is not an experienced traveler—or if he simply wants to be confident that his trip will hold as few unpleasant surprises as possible—he may wish to call upon the services of a reputable travel agent.

Not only should a seasoned travel agent handle a gentleman's travel and lodging requests, while keeping an eye on the gentleman's vacation budget, but he should also be able to provide information about the culture and traditions of the cities the gentleman hopes to visit. A good travel agent is armed with a wealth of advice, including helpful information about various hotels and the sometimes tricky business of making air, train, and bus connections in hard-to-get-to cities. A well-

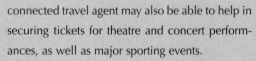

connected travel agent may also be able to help in securing tickets for theatre and concert performances, as well as major sporting events.

What's more, with travel regulations changing on an almost weekly basis, a dependable travel agent will be able to provide a gentleman with accurate updates as to the rules and restrictions he may expect to encounter. Given the availability of e-mail and cell phones, a responsible travel agent will also be able to assist a gentleman should he encounter unforeseen difficulties over the course of his trip.

A gentleman need not engage a travel agency to handle every detail of his trip. It is bad form, however, for him to lead the travel agent on, asking for detailed information and then proceeding to book his travel on his own.

Experienced, dependable travel agents are frequently certified by the Travel Institute. A gentleman may wish to take his business to an agent whom the institute lists as a Certified Travel Agent (CTA) or a Certified Travel Counselor (CTC). A list of Travel Institute–certified agents is available online at www.thetravelinstitute.com.

COPENHAGEN, DENMARK

The beloved sculpture of the Little Mermaid keeps her gentle, melancholy watch in the harbor of this timeless city. If a gentleman wants the Danes to love him, he will be sure to say "Copen-HAY-gen," not "Copen-HAH-gen." English will be understood as a second language—or almost a first one—virtually everywhere.

DISTANCE FROM OTHER CITIES

220 miles from Berlin

301 miles from Oslo

324 miles from Stockholm

3,847 miles from New York

4,257 miles from Chicago

5,602 miles from Los Angeles

AVERAGE MONTHLY TEMPERATURE

Month	Low	High
January	30	37
February	28	36
March	32	41
April	36	49
May	45	60

Month	Low	High
June	52	66
July	55	69
August	54	69
September	50	61
October	44	53
November	37	44
December	32	39

TIME DIFFERENCE

When it is 10:00 a.m. in Copenhagen . . .

it is 4:00 a.m. in New York

it is 3:00 a.m. in Chicago

it is 1:00 a.m. in Los Angeles

AMERICAN EMBASSY

Dag Hammarskjölds Allé 24

2100 København Ø

Copenhagen, Denmark

Telephone: +45 33-41-71-00

Fax: +45 35-43-02-23

CURRENCY

Krone

DRIVING

A gentleman drives on the right side of the road.

ELECTRICITY

230 V   50 Hz

TIPPING

Restaurants: A service charge is generally included with each bill. No further tip is necessary unless a gentleman feels he has received exceptional service.

Cabs: No tip is necessary.

Hotel assistance: 5 kroner per bag

GENTLEMANLY PHRASES

English	Danish
Hello	Goddag
Good-bye	Farvel
Thank you	Tak
You're welcome	Selv tak
Good morning	Godmorgen
Good night	Godnat
Yes	Ja
No	Nej
Excuse me	Undskyld

English	Danish
Pleased to meet you	Det glader mig at mode
How are you?	Hvordan har du det?
Fine, thanks	Godt tak
I don't understand	Jeg forstår ikke
English	Engelsk

TRADITIONAL TOAST

Skaal

———

An informed gentleman knows that if he has been invited to dinner by a Dane, he should refrain from drinking until his host has made a toast.

Dublin, Ireland

Dublin is not all about pubs, but its pubs are a good place to start. They're also a splendid place to end the day after an evening at the theatre. Congenial conversation will be forthcoming, rest assured.

Distance from Other Cities

109 miles from Limerick

136 miles from Cork

287 miles from London

3,179 miles from New York

3,666 miles from Chicago

5,168 miles from Los Angeles

Average Monthly Temperature

Month	Low	High
January	37	46
February	37	46
March	38	49
April	40	53
May	44	58
June	49	63
July	53	66

Month	Low	High
August	52	66
September	49	62
October	46	57
November	40	50
December	38	57

TIME DIFFERENCE

When it is 10:00 a.m. in Dublin . . .

it is 5:00 a.m. in New York

it is 4:00 a.m. in Chicago

it is 2:00 a.m. in Los Angeles

AMERICAN EMBASSY

42 Elgin Road

Ballsbridge

Dublin 4, Ireland

Telephone: +353 1-668-8777

Fax: +353 1-668-9946

CURRENCY

Euro

DRIVING

A gentleman drives on the left side of the road.

ELECTRICITY

230 V   50 Hz

TIPPING

Restaurants: A gentleman leaves a 10%–15% tip when a service charge hasn't been included.

Cab: A gentleman leaves a tip of 10% of the fare.

Hotel assistance: 1 euro per bag

GENTLEMANLY PHRASES

Note: The main language spoken in Ireland, especially in Dublin, is English. However, in some parts of the country, particularly the western coast of Ireland, Gaelic is still spoken at times.

English	*Gaelic*
Hello	Dia duit
Good-bye	Slán
Please	Más é do thoil é
Thank you	Go raibh maith agat
Good morning	Maidin mhaith
Good night	Olche mhaith
Yes	Sea
No	Ní hea
Excuse me	Gabh mo leithscéal

English	*Gaelic*
How are you?	Conas atá tú?
Fine	Támé
I don't understand	Ní thuigim
English	Béarla

TRADITIONAL TOAST
Sláinte

An informed gentleman knows that, in Ireland, if someone is kind enough to buy him a drink, he is expected to be kind enough to return the favor.

EDINBURGH, SCOTLAND

Ghosts are said to haunt Scotland's castles, highlands, and lowlands, while Edinburgh itself remains one of the loveliest, best-preserved cities in the British Isles. The Scots may not be as forthcoming as the Irish, but over a pot of ale, they're likely to tell you a tale.

DISTANCE FROM OTHER CITIES

24 miles from Glasgow

30 miles from St. Andrews

330 miles from Paris

3,260 miles from New York

3,710 miles from Chicago

5,154 miles from Los Angeles

AVERAGE MONTHLY TEMPERATURE

Month	Low	High
January	32	43
February	32	43
March	34	47
April	37	52
May	42	57
June	47	63

Month	Low	High
July	50	65
August	50	65
September	47	61
October	42	55
November	35	47
December	33	44

TIME DIFFERENCE

When it is 10:00 a.m. in Edinburgh . . .

it is 5:00 a.m. in New York

it is 4:00 a.m. in Chicago

it is 2:00 a.m. in Los Angeles

AMERICAN EMBASSY

The American embassy in London handles all matters for Scotland.

4 Grosvenor Square
London, W1A 1AE
United Kingdom
Telephone: +44 020-7499-9000

CURRENCY

Pound

DRIVING

A gentleman drives on the left side of the road.

ELECTRICITY

230 V   50 Hz

TIPPING

Restaurants: A gentleman leaves a tip of 10% of the bill, unless a service charge has already been added.

Cabs: A gentleman leaves a tip of 10% of the fare.

Hotel assistance: 1 pound per bag

SCOTTISH PHRASES

Scottish	*American*
Billy	Boy
Bonny	Beautiful
Brough	Town
Couthie	Pleasant
Kirk	Church
Lass	Girl
Wee	Small

TRADITIONAL TOAST

Shlante

An informed gentleman does not refer to the people of Scotland as Scotch. He is aware that they are Scottish or Scots; Scotch is normally used only in reference to whiskey or dishes such as Scotch eggs.

ROOMS FOR RENT

When a gentleman is traveling abroad, he makes sure to reserve his lodgings well ahead of time. (If he is traveling to a major tourist destination at peak season, he will be smart to start making his reservations as much as six months in advance.) He may choose to stay in a grand hotel or in more modest digs. In some cities he may be able to find a charming little bed-and-breakfast; in the countryside he may enjoy the delights of a rustic inn.

If his tastes run to the luxurious, a gentleman may wish to book his stay at a well-known, distinguished hotel. If he is concerned about the dependability of the service he will be offered, he may wish to stick to hotels that are part of an international chain. On the other hand, if he only plans to be in his hotel room for the few hours he will be sleeping, he may wish to opt for lodgings that are decidedly simpler, and more economical, as well.

If a gentleman is adept at using the Internet, he may feel confident in his own abilities to scout out a great bargain and handle his own reservations. He will want to investigate the reputation and the realities of any hotel, however—no matter what its

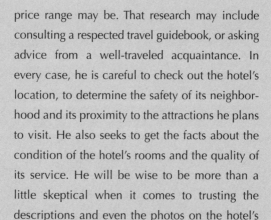

price range may be. That research may include consulting a respected travel guidebook, or asking advice from a well-traveled acquaintance. In every case, he is careful to check out the hotel's location, to determine the safety of its neighborhood and its proximity to the attractions he plans to visit. He also seeks to get the facts about the condition of the hotel's rooms and the quality of its service. He will be wise to be more than a little skeptical when it comes to trusting the descriptions and even the photos on the hotel's Web site.

If a gentleman is anxious about the quality of his lodgings, he may wish to book them through a reputable travel agent, who will be able to help him secure the sort of room he wishes, at a price that at least comes close to fitting his budget.

In many instances, his hotel may offer him the option of the "American Plan" or the "European Plan." The American Plan includes three meals a day, while the European Plan includes only the hotel room. The American Plan offers a certain level of convenience, provided a traveler is content to take all his meals in the same dining room every day. If he plans to spend as little time as possible in his hotel room, the European Plan is almost certain to be the more attractive option.

A well-informed gentleman understands that, when he is traveling abroad, he is likely to encounter hotel rooms that are less than spacious, even in the best hotels. In smaller hotels, he may find that the heating is idiosyncratic and that there is no air-conditioning at all. He may even find himself making a midnight trek to a shared bathroom, located at the end of the hall. If a gentleman is not amused by these sorts of surprises, he must be especially diligent in his hotel research.

HONG KONG, CHINA

Lanterns twinkle in the twilight, dragons twist and twine their way through the streets, and the crackling of fireworks fills the air. From the Chinese New Year Festival on through the Winter Solstice, this is a city of celebrations. Expect a spectacle almost every day.

DISTANCE FROM OTHER CITIES

499 miles from Taipei

755 miles from Shanghai

1,225 miles from Beijing

7,247 miles from Los Angeles

7,798 miles from Chicago

8,059 miles from New York

AVERAGE MONTHLY TEMPERATURE

Month	Low	High
January	58	67
February	59	67
March	63	71
April	69	77
May	75	83
June	79	86

Month	Low	High
July	81	89
August	81	89
September	79	87
October	75	83
November	67	76
December	60	70

TIME DIFFERENCE

When it is 10:00 a.m. in Hong Kong . . .

it is 10:00 p.m. the previous day in
New York

it is 9:00 p.m. the previous day in Chicago

it is 7:00 p.m. the previous day in
Los Angeles

AMERICAN CONSULATE

26 Garden Road
Hong Kong
Telephone: +852 2523-9011
Fax: +852 2845-1598

CURRENCY

Hong Kong dollar

DRIVING

A gentleman drives on the left side of the road.

ELECTRICITY

220 V   50 Hz

TIPPING

Restaurants: A gentleman leaves a tip of 10% of the bill, even if there is a service charge.

Cabs: A gentleman leaves a tip by rounding up the fare to the nearest Hong Kong dollar.

Hotel assistance: 5 Hong Kong dollars per bag

GENTLEMANLY PHRASES

English	Chinese
Hello	Ninhao
Good-bye	Zaijian
Please	Qing
Thank you	Xiexie
You're welcome	Bu xie
Good morning	Nin zao
Good night	Wan an
Yes	Shi
No	Bu
Excuse me	Duibuqi
How are you?	Ni hao ma?

English	Chinese
English	*Chinese*
Fine, thank you	Hao xiexie
I don't understand	Wo bu dong
English	Yingwen

TRADITIONAL TOAST

Ganbei

An informed gentleman knows that Hong Kong is a shopper's paradise. If he plans to make shopping a part of his trip, he must also have a plan for getting his purchases home.

JERUSALEM, ISRAEL

The sacred city of three major religions,
Jerusalem remains a place of controversy. A visit
to the Shrine at Bethlehem may be arranged,
however, as may an opportunity to pause
respectfully at the Wailing Wall. Provided he
makes the proper arrangements ahead of time, a
gentleman may experience the deeply moving
sites of Jerusalem without fear for his safety.

DISTANCE FROM OTHER CITIES
    34 miles from Tel Aviv
    73 miles from Haifa
    264 miles from Cairo
    5,701 miles from New York
    6,195 miles from Chicago
    7,582 miles from Los Angeles

AVERAGE MONTHLY TEMPERATURE

Month	Low	High
January	39	53
February	40	56
March	43	61
April	49	70

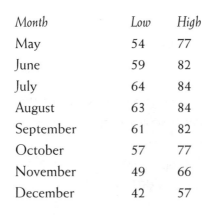

Month	Low	High
May	54	77
June	59	82
July	64	84
August	63	84
September	61	82
October	57	77
November	49	66
December	42	57

TIME DIFFERENCE

When it is 10:00 a.m. in Jerusalem . . .

it is 3:00 a.m. in New York

it is 2:00 a.m. in Chicago

it is midnight in Los Angeles

AMERICAN EMBASSY

71 Hayarkon Street
Tel Aviv 63903, Israel
Telephone: +972 3-519575

CURRENCY

New Israel shekel

DRIVING

A gentleman drives on the right side of the road.

ELECTRICITY

230 V   50 Hz

TIPPING

Restaurants: A gentleman leaves a tip of 10% of the bill, unless a service charge has already been added.

Cabs: No tip is necessary.

Hotel assistance: 2–3 shekels per bag

GENTLEMANLY PHRASES

English	Hebrew
Hello	Shalom
Good-bye	Shalom
Please	Bevakusha
Thank you	Toda
You're welcome	Al lo davar
Good morning	Boker tov
Good night	Lilah tov
Yes	Ken
No	Lo
Excuse me	Slekah
Pleased to meet you	Nayim mayod
How are you?	Ma shlomecha?
Fine, thanks	Tov, todah

English	Hebrew
English	*Hebrew*
I don't understand	Ani lo mevin
English	Angleet

TRADITIONAL TOAST
L'chaim

An informed gentleman knows that in Israel he may encounter security checks at the entrance to stores. He realizes that being frisked by a security guard before entering a shopping mall is an everyday occurrence in Jerusalem, as well as in many other major cities outside the United States, so he isn't alarmed.

LISBON, PORTUGAL

The weather is well nigh perfect almost any time of the year, in the city or on its white-sand beaches. The shore provides a languorous retreat from the busy city itself, where the sounds of Lisbon's popular music, *fado*, fills the night air.

DISTANCE FROM OTHER CITIES

170 miles from Porto

313 miles from Madrid

903 miles from Paris

3,371 miles from New York

3,997 miles from Chicago

5,676 miles from Los Angeles

AVERAGE MONTHLY TEMPERATURE

Month	Low	High
January	46	58
February	48	60
March	49	63
April	52	66
May	55	71
June	60	76
July	63	81

Month	Low	High
August	63	82
September	62	70
October	58	72
November	52	64
December	48	58

TIME DIFFERENCE

When it is 10:00 a.m. in Lisbon . . .

it is 5:00 a.m. in New York

it is 4:00 a.m. in Chicago

it is 2:00 a.m. in Los Angeles

AMERICAN EMBASSY

Avenida das Forças Armadas

1600-081 Lisboa, Portugal

Telephone: +351 21-727-3300

Fax: +351 21-726-9109

CURRENCY

Euro

DRIVING

A gentleman drives on the right side of the road.

Electricity

230 V   50 Hz

Tipping

Restaurants: A gentleman leaves a tip of 5%–10% of the bill, in addition to the service charge.

Cabs: A gentleman leaves a tip of 10% of the fare.

Hotel assistance: 1 euro per bag

Gentlemanly Phrases

English	Portuguese
Hello	Olá
Good-bye	Adeus
Please	Por favor
Thank you	Obrigado
You're welcome	De nadah
Good morning	Bom dia
Good night	Boa noite
Yes	Sim
No	Não
Excuse me	Cum licenca
How are you?	Como está?
Fine, thanks	Bem, obrigado

| I don't understand | Não compreendo |
| English | Inglês |

TRADITIONAL TOAST
A sua suade

―――

An informed gentleman knows that Lisbon is known as the city of seven hills. If he plans on trekking up those hills, he wears comfortable shoes.

WAIT A MINUTE!
WHO SAYS I WEAR A 54?

UNDERSTANDING THE
EUROPEAN SIZE CHART

As more and more clothing is manufactured in Europe—or as more and more clothing manufacturers seem to wish to give that impression—a gentleman may be asked to try on garments labeled with unfamiliar sizes, most of them much larger than anything he has ever tried on before. A gentleman need not be alarmed. A single chart will help him understand the correlations:

HATS

USA	Europe
6	54
7	56
7¼	58
7½	60
7¾	62

Shirts

USA/UK	Europe
14	36
14½	37
15	38
15½	39
16	41
16½	42
17	43
17½	44
18	45

Shoes

USA	UK	Europe
7	6½	40
7½	7	40½
8	7½	41
8½	8	42
9	8½	42½
9½	9	43
10	9½	44
10½	10	44½
11	10½	45
11½	11	46
12	11½	46½

UNDERSTANDING THE EUROPEAN SIZING CHART

Suits

USA/UK	Europe
36	46
38	48
40	50
42	52
44	54
46	56
48	58

Underwear

USA	Europe
34	5
36	6
38	7
40	8
42	9
44	10
46	11
48	12

London, England

Not every day in London is a foggy day. But even if the weather is less than pleasant, there will always be grand art museums, lovely parks, and fine shopping for shirts, suits, and ties.

Distance from Other Cities

163 miles from Manchester

213 miles from Paris

333 miles from Glasgow

463 miles from New York

3,954 miles from Chicago

5,448 miles from Los Angeles

Average Monthly Temperature

Month	Low	High
January	32	44
February	32	44
March	34	49
April	38	54
May	43	61
June	48	67
July	52	71
August	51	70

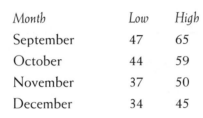

Month	Low	High
September	47	65
October	44	59
November	37	50
December	34	45

Time Difference

When it is 10:00 a.m. in London . . .

it is 5:00 a.m. in New York

it is 4:00 a.m. in Chicago

it is 2:00 a.m. in Los Angeles

American Embassy

24 Grosvenor Square

London, W1A 1AE

United Kingdom

Telephone: +44 0-20-7499-9000

Currency

Pound

Driving

A gentleman drives on the left side of the road.

Electricity

240 V   50 Hz

Tipping

Restaurants: If a service charge has not been added, a gentleman leaves a tip of approximately 10% of the bill.

Cabs: A gentleman leaves a tip of 10% of the fare.

Hotel assistance: 1 pound per bag

British Phrases

British	*American*
Bank holiday	National holiday
Biscuit	Cookie
Chemist	Pharmacist
Gents	Men's room
Jacket potato	Baked potato
Jumper	Sweater
Knickers	Panties
Lift	Elevator
Loo	Bathroom
Pub	Bar
Queue	Line
Underground	Subway
Waistcoat	Vest

TRADITIONAL TOAST
Cheers

———

An informed gentleman knows that many of the more popular tourist attractions in London are only open to the public during certain months of each year. If a visit to such sites is important to him, a gentleman checks their days of operation before making his travel arrangements.

Madrid, Spain

Spain's monarchs were traditionally buried in the Escurial. Their portraits hang in the Prado. And yes, for the most part, this major city takes a breather every afternoon at siesta-time. But don't worry about losing your sightseeing time. Supper often doesn't start until nine.

Distance from Other Cities

291 miles from Ibiza

313 miles from Lisbon

314 miles from Barcelona

3,587 miles from New York

4,186 miles from Chicago

5,827 miles from Los Angeles

Average Monthly Temperature

Month	Low	High
January	32	51
February	35	54
March	38	60
April	42	63
May	48	71
June	56	82

Month	Low	High
July	61	90
August	61	90
September	55	82
October	47	68
November	39	58
December	35	52

TIME DIFFERENCE

When it is 10:00 a.m. in Madrid . . .

it is 4:00 a.m. in New York

it is 3:00 a.m. in Chicago

it is 1:00 a.m. in Los Angeles

AMERICAN EMBASSY

Calle Serrano 75

28006 Madrid, Spain

Telephone: +34 91-587-2240

Fax: +34 91-587-2243

CURRENCY

Euro

DRIVING

A gentleman drives on the right side of the road.

Electricity

230 V   50 Hz

Tipping

Restaurants: A gentleman adds a tip of 10% of the bill.

Cabs: For a metered trip, a gentleman adds 10% to the fare. If the fare is not metered, there is no need to add a tip.

Hotel assistance: 1 euro per bag

Gentlemanly Phrases

English	Spanish
Hello	Hola
Good-bye	Adiós
Please	Por favor
Thank you	Gracias
You're welcome	De nada
Good morning	Buenos días
Good night	Buenas noches
Yes	Sí
No	No
Excuse me	Con permiso
Pleased to meet you	Mucho gusto
How are you?	¿Cómo está usted?

English	Spanish
Fine, thanks	Bien, gracia
I don't understand	No entiendo
English	Inglés

TRADITIONAL TOAST
Salud

An informed gentleman knows that a siesta is the norm with many businesses in Madrid. He keeps that in mind when making his afternoon plans.

MANILA, PHILIPPINES

It was the sixteenth-century Spanish who built
the Intramuros, the walled city that still sits at
the heart of Manila. But the city was originally
settled by Muslims, and after the Spanish the
English ruled. Vestiges of all these cultures
remain, as do some of the mangrove trees that
gave Manila its name. Be sure to engage a guide
who speaks the native language, Tagalog. You
may not hear much English on the streets.

DISTANCE FROM OTHER CITIES
355 miles from Cebu
606 miles from Davao
696 miles from Hong Kong
7,302 miles from Los Angeles
8,138 miles from Chicago
8,504 mles from New York

AVERAGE MONTHLY TEMPERATURE

Month	Low	High
January	71	86
February	72	88
March	73	90
April	76	93

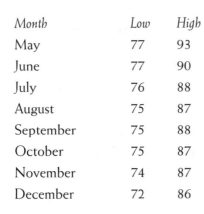

Month	Low	High
May	77	93
June	77	90
July	76	88
August	75	87
September	75	88
October	75	87
November	74	87
December	72	86

TIME DIFFERENCE

When it is 10:00 a.m. in Manila . . .

it is 10:00 p.m. the previous day in
New York

it is 9:00 p.m. the previous day in Chicago

it is 7:00 p.m. the previous day in
Los Angeles

AMERICAN EMBASSY

1201 Roxas Boulevard

Manila, Philippines 1000

Telephone: +63 2-528-6300,
extension 2555, 2246

Fax : +63 2-522-3242

CURRENCY
Peso

DRIVING
A gentleman drives on the right side of the road.

ELECTRICITY
220 V   60 Hz

TIPPING
Restaurants: A gentleman leaves a tip of 10% of the bill.

Cabs: A gentleman leaves a tip of 10% of the fare.

Hotel assistance: 50 pesos per bag

GENTLEMANLY PHRASES

English	*Tagalog*
Hello	Mabuhay
Good-bye	Paalam
Please	Paki
Thank you	Salamat
You're welcome	Walang anuman
Good morning	Magandang umaga
Good night	Magandang gabi
Yes	Oo

English	Tagalog
English	*Tagalog*
No	Hindi
Excuse me	Paumanhin
Pleased to meet you	Ikinagagalak kong makilala ka
How are you?	Kamusta ka?
Fine, thanks	Mabuti naman, salamat
I don't understand	Hindi ko maintindihan
English	Ingles

TRADITIONAL TOAST

Mabuhay

An informed gentleman knows he never leaves his hotel in Manila without an umbrella.

Dollars and Sense

Shortly before a gentleman sets out on a trip abroad, he visits his bank. There he purchases a small number of bills and coins in the currency of the country he is visiting—just enough to get him through the airport and into his hotel.

As a general rule, it is more expensive to buy foreign currency in the United States. The transaction can be made at a lower cost on foreign soil. When he is departing from a foreign country, a gentleman will also be well advised to divest himself of all local bills and coins, since, as a general rule, he will be able to make no use of them once he returns home.

Once he has arrived at his hotel, a gentleman sits down and familiarizes himself with the currency of the place he is visiting. Consulting a reputable travel guidebook, he sits down and places the various bills and coins before him and does his best to understand them.

He also acquaints himself with the most convenient *bureau de change* (pronounced "bewrow duh shange"), where he usually will get the best exchange rate for his U.S. dollars. He never exchanges his dollars for local currency on the street.

In most restaurants and department stores, a gentleman will be able to use his credit card. In street-side markets and in small boutiques, however, he will have no option other than to pay cash. Unless he has become especially adept in handling the local currency, he may find himself with no recourse other than to offer the merchant a handful of coins, in hopes that he will get the right change in return.

A gentleman attempts to acquaint himself with the local currency, no matter what. Otherwise, he will come home with pockets bulging with virtually useless coins.

Mexico City, Mexico

Dating from the mid-sixteenth century, Mexico City is the oldest city in North America, but its pre-Spanish history goes back even farther than that. Although museums and galleries abound, a gentleman will be wise to spend plenty of time on the plazas, since the weather is almost perfect, virtually year round

Distance from Other Cities

183 miles from Acapulco

733 miles from Cabo San Lucas

405 miles from Puerto Vallarta

1,551 miles from Los Angeles

1,693 miles from Chicago

2,094 miles from New York

Average Monthly Temperature

Month	Low	High
January	43	70
February	45	73
March	49	77
April	52	79
May	54	79

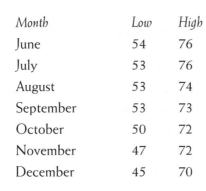

Month	Low	High
June	54	76
July	53	76
August	53	74
September	53	73
October	50	72
November	47	72
December	45	70

TIME DIFFERENCE

When it is 10:00 a.m. in Mexico City . . .

it is 11:00 a.m. in New York

it is 10:00 a.m. in Chicago

it is 8:00 a.m. in Los Angeles

AMERICAN EMBASSY

Paseo de la Reforma 305
Col. Cuauhtemoc
06500 Mexico, D.F.
Telephone: +52 55-5080-2000
Fax: +52 55-5511-9980

CURRENCY

Peso

DRIVING

A gentleman drives on the right side of the road.

ELECTRICITY

127 V   60 Hz

TIPPING

Restaurants: A gentleman leaves a tip of 10%–15% of the bill.

Cabs: As cabs are not generally metered in Mexico, it is not customary for a gentleman to tip a driver.

Hotel assistance: 10 pesos per bag

GENTLEMANLY PHRASES

English	*Spanish*
Hello	Hola
Good-bye	Adiós
Please	Por favor
Thank you	Gracias
You're welcome	De nada
Good morning	Buenos días
Good night	Buenas noches
Yes	Sí
No	No
Excuse me	Con permiso

English	Spanish
Pleased to meet you	Mucho gusto
How are you?	¿Cómo está usted?
Fine, thanks	Bien, gracias
I don't understand	No entiendo
English	Inglés

TRADITIONAL TOAST
Salud

An informed gentleman never hails taxis on the street in Mexico City. He only takes cabs operating from taxi stands or cabs called for him by hotel or restaurant staff.

Monte Carlo

Tiny, and glamorous beyond words, Monte Carlo was—and still is—the playground of the extremely rich and the extremely beautiful. Every other haven of the high life pales by comparison. Take care in the casinos, however, lest you lose your designer shirt.

Distance from Other Cities
31 miles from Cannes

257 miles from Zurich

595 miles from Paris

3,996 miles from New York

4,535 miles from Chicago

6,075 miles from Los Angeles

Average Monthly Temperature

Month	Low	High
January	50	58
February	50	60
March	54	62
April	58	66
May	64	72
June	72	80

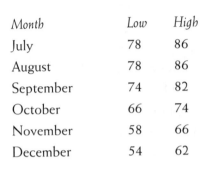

Month	Low	High
July	78	86
August	78	86
September	74	82
October	66	74
November	58	66
December	54	62

TIME DIFFERENCE

When it is 10:00 a.m. in Monte Carlo . . .

it is 4:00 a.m. in New York

it is 3:00 a.m. in Chicago

it is 1:00 a.m. in Los Angeles

AMERICAN EMBASSY

The closest office is located in Marseille, France.

Place Varian Fry

13286 Marseille Cedex 6, France

Telephone: +33 4-91-54-92-00

CURRENCY

Euro

DRIVING

A gentleman drives on the right side of the road.

ELECTRICITY

127/220 V   50 Hz

TIPPING

Restaurants: As a rule, restaurant checks in Monte Carlo include a 15% service fee. If a gentleman has received exceptional service, he may wish to leave an additional 5%–10%.

Cabs: A gentleman leaves a tip of 5%–10% of his fare.

Hotel assistance: 1 euro per bag

GENTLEMANLY PHRASES

English	French
Hello	Bonjour
Good-bye	Au revoir
Please	S'il vous plaît
Thank you	Merci
You're welcome	De rien
Good morning	Bonjour
Good night	Bonsoir
Yes	Oui
No	Non
Excuse me	Pardonnez-moi
Pleased to meet you	Enchanté

English	*French*
How are you?	Comment allez-vous?
Fine , thanks	Bien, merci
I don't understand	Je ne comprends pas
English	Anglais

TRADITIONAL TOAST

A votre santé

An informed gentleman knows that in Monte Carlo, appropriate clothing must be worn in all public establishments, especially in houses of worship. For receptions or the casino, a jacket and tie should be worn. For gala events, a tuxedo is de rigueur.

MONTREAL, CANADA

Almost every major language is spoken in Montreal, one of the world's most cosmopolitan cities. Art and music abound within this New World city with an Old World ambience.

DISTANCE FROM OTHER CITIES

    314 miles from Toronto

    329 miles from New York

    747 miles from Chicago

    1,878 miles from Calgary

    2,293 miles from Vancouver

    2,469 miles from Los Angeles

AVERAGE MONTHLY TEMPERATURE

Month	Low	High
January	5	21
February	7	24
March	19	35
April	33	51
May	45	65
June	54	74
July	59	79
August	57	76

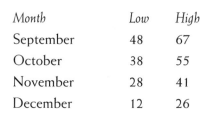

Month	Low	High
September	48	67
October	38	55
November	28	41
December	12	26

TIME DIFFERENCE

If it is 10:00 a.m. in Montreal . . .

it is 10:00 a.m. in New York

it is 9:00 a.m. in Chicago

it is 7:00 a.m. in Los Angeles

AMERICAN CONSULATE

1155 rue Saint-Alexandre

Montreal, QC H3B 3Z1 Canada

Telephone: +514 398-9695

Fax: +514 398-0975

CURRENCY

Canadian dollar

DRIVING

A gentleman drives on the right side of the road.

ELECTRICITY

120 V   60 Hz

TIPPING

Restaurants: A gentleman leaves a tip equal to 15%–20% of the bill.

Cabs: A gentleman leaves a tip of 15% of the fare.

Hotel assistance: 1–2 Canadian dollars per bag

GENTLEMANLY PHRASES

English	*French*
Hello	Bonjour
Good-bye	Au revoir
Please	S'il vous plaît
Thank you	Merci
You're welcome	De rien
Good morning	Bonjour
Good night	Bonne nuit
Yes	Oui
No	Non
Excuse me	Pardonnez-moi
Pleased to meet you	Enchanté
How are you?	Comment allez-vous?
Fine, thanks	Bien, merci
I don't understand	Je ne comprends pas
English	Anglais

TRADITIONAL TOAST
A votre santé

———

An informed gentleman knows that Canada is a bilingual country, so he should be prepared to see all signage in both French and English. He is never afraid to ask for help in English, of course.

Oslo, Norway

Of course, you can visit a Viking ship in Oslo, but you can also visit Thor Heyerdahl's legendary raft, the *Kon-Tiki*. Oslo's citizens are some of the best educated in the world, and some of the most cosmopolitan. You won't need a Norwegian phrase book. Even the bars have English names.

Distance from Other Cities

189 miles from Bergen

258 miles from Stockholm

489 miles from Helsinki

3,676 miles from New York

4,044 miles from Chicago

5,334 miles from Los Angeles

Average Monthly Temperature

Month	Low	High
January	20	31
February	19	32
March	27	39
April	34	49
May	45	62
June	52	68

Month	Low	High
July	55	71
August	53	69
September	45	60
October	38	49
November	29	39
December	22	32

TIME DIFFERENCE

When it is 10:00 a.m. in Oslo . . .

it is 4:00 a.m. in New York

it is 3:00 a.m. in Chicago

it is 1:00 a.m. in Los Angeles

AMERICAN EMBASSY

Henrik Ibsens gate 48

0244 Oslo, Norway

Telehone: +47 22-44-85-50

CURRENCY

Krone

DRIVING

A gentleman drives on the right side of the road.

Electricity

230 V   50 Hz

Tipping

Restaurants: Tips are generally included as a service charge. A gentleman adds an additional 5% if the service was exceptional.

Cabs: A gentleman leaves a tip of 10% of the fare.

Hotel assistance: 5 kroner per bag

Gentlemanly Phrases

English	Norwegian
Hello	Hei
Good-bye	Hadet
Please	Vær så snill
Thank you	Tusen takk
You're welcome	Bare hyggelig
Good morning	God morgen
Good night	God natt
Yes	Ja
No	Nei
Excuse me	Unnskyld
Pleased to meet you	Hyggelig å treffe deg
How are you?	Hvordan går det?

English	Norwegian
Fine, thanks	Takk, bare bra
I don't understand	Jeg forstår ikke
English	Engelsk

TRADITIONAL TOAST
Skaal

An informed gentleman knows that Oslo's nightlife can be a very expensive proposition. A night out on the town can prove to be a budget-breaking experience if he is not careful.

Unfamiliar Entrées

Foreign travel not only provides a gentleman with the opportunity to visit fabled sights and see legendary works of art, but also gives him the chance to experience the diverse, and frequently delightful, cuisines of other countries.

A gentleman looks forward to every meal in a different country—whether it is a sandwich picked up at a sidewalk market, a quick lunch at an open-air café, or a grandiose dinner at a splendid restaurant—as a new experience, one to be cherished in his memory.

However, unless he is fluent in the local language, a gentleman may find himself stymied when presented with a menu in a foreign city. Fortunately, if he is wise, before entering a restaurant, he will have equipped himself with a few handy phrases. He knows how to begin the meal by saying, "Good morning," "Good day," or "Good evening." He knows how to say, "Do you speak English?" And, most important of all, he knows how to say, "Please" and "Thank you."

In most major cities, the server—or somebody else in the restaurant—will have at least a passing knowledge of English. A gentleman would never be so presumptuous, however, as to expect this to be the case. Instead, he carries with him a translation guide that will help him understand what he is being offered and what he may be ordering. (He is not ashamed to pull out his translation guide at the table.)

Once the gentleman and the server have come to terms as to their understanding of each other's languages, he asks for the server's recommendations from the menu. (In many countries, the servers take great pride, and even have a proprietary interest, in the offerings on their menu. They consider it a gesture of respect when the guest asks them for their advice.)

The gentleman then proceeds to place his order, pointing to items on the menu or using other sign language, as required. Should his meal arrive and turn out not to be what he expected, he respectfully explains this fact to the server and asks for something else. (A gentleman never feels so intimidated that he will eat food that might make him ill, either at home or abroad.)

When his server refills his glass, replaces a piece of flatware, or assists him in any way, a gentleman always says, "thank you," even if he

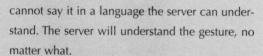

cannot say it in a language the server can understand. The server will understand the gesture, no
matter what.

If a gentleman is less than adventurous in his
choice of food, or if his digestive system is a trifle
unpredictable, he may wish to stick to fare that is
familiar to him. If fish and chips, a gyros sandwich,
a slice of pizza, or a simple dish of pasta seems to
him like the safest option, that is what he orders. If
other travelers, or his doctor, have advised him not
to drink the local tap water, he sticks with the
bottled kind and drinks it at room temperature,
remembering that local ice cubes have been made
from local water.

At the close of his meal, when he settles his tab,
a gentleman will be expected to leave a tip. In most
major cities, where his credit card is accepted, he
may simply add the "service charge" to his bill, as
he would do in the United States. If the restaurant
or café is on a cash-only basis, he leaves his tip as
cash, on the table—or on the saucer left for that
purpose by the server.

A tip of 20 percent is exorbitant by some local
standards, but if a gentleman leaves that percent-
age, especially when he is unfamiliar with the local

customs, he will be sure that he has done the right thing. He would never be so condescending as to think that a few coins, tossed in the dish, will be "enough," simply because he does not understand the local currency.

In many countries, a gentleman will also be expected to give a few coins to the person who helps him with his coat at the coat-check, a couple of bills to the host who leads him to his table, and a few coins to the person who ushers him out the door, especially if he is being ushered into a cab. (In all cases, these tips will be pretty much the same as the gentleman would give in the United States.)

A gentleman never frets about over-tipping. If the server is prohibited from accepting tips, he will say that such is the case, and the gentleman will say, "thank you," and move on.

PARIS, FRANCE

The City of Lights is misty in the autumn, but full of flowers in the spring. Paris is about memorable food and legendary art. If you want to visit the Louvre, especially if there's a major exhibition, check to see if you'll need reservations. Otherwise, you may miss the *Mona Lisa*.

DISTANCE FROM OTHER CITIES

213 miles from London

411 miles from Marseille

687 miles from Rome

3,628 miles from New York

4,138 miles from Chicago

5,653 miles from Los Angeles

AVERAGE MONTHLY TEMPERATURE

Month	Low	High
January	34	43
February	34	45
March	38	51
April	42	57
May	49	64
June	54	70

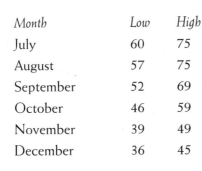

Month	Low	High
July	60	75
August	57	75
September	52	69
October	46	59
November	39	49
December	36	45

Time Difference

If it is 10.00 a.m. in Paris . . .

> it is 4:00 a.m. in New York
>
> it is 3:00 a.m. in Chicago
>
> it is 1:00 a.m. in Los Angeles

American Embassy

2 avenue Gabriel

75382 Paris Cedex 08, France

Telephone: +33 1-43-12-22-22

Fax: +33 1-42-66-97-83

Currency

Euro

Driving

A gentleman drives on the right side of the road.

Electricity

230 V 50 Hz

Tipping

Restaurants: As a rule, Parisian restaurant checks include a 15% service fee. If a gentleman has received exceptional service, he may wish to leave an additional 5%–10%.

Cabs: A gentleman tips his cab driver 5%–10% of the fare.

Hotel assistance: 1 euro per bag

Gentlemanly Phrases

English	French
Hello	Bonjour
Good-bye	Au revoir
Please	S'il vous plaît
Thank you	Merci
You're welcome	De rien
Good morning	Bonjour
Good night	Bonne nuit
Yes	Oui
No	Non
Excuse me	Pardonnez-moi
Pleased to meet you	Enchanté

English	French
How are you?	Comment allez-vous?
Fine , thanks	Bien, merci
I don't understand	Je ne comprends pas
English	Anglais

TRADITIONAL TOAST

A votre santé

If eating at a particular restaurant in Paris—especially a well-known one—is critical to a gentleman's enjoyment of his trip, he knows to make his reservation well ahead of time.

PRAGUE, CZECH REPUBLIC

It's known as Golden Prague because its gilded palaces still gleam, having escaped the ravages of World War II. Don't miss the Prague Castle or the Jewish Quarter, both of which still teach us lessons about the triumphs and struggles of generations past.

DISTANCE FROM OTHER CITIES

114 miles from Brno

156 miles from Vienna

174 miles from Berlin

4,086 miles from New York

4,544 miles from Chicago

5,953 miles from Los Angeles

AVERAGE MONTHLY TEMPERATURE

Month	Low	High
January	24	34
February	25	36
March	32	46
April	36	54
May	45	64
June	51	69

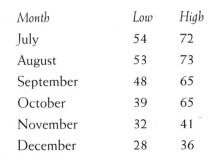

Month	Low	High
July	54	72
August	53	73
September	48	65
October	39	65
November	32	41
December	28	36

TIME DIFFERENCE

When it is 10:00 a.m. in Prague . . .

it is 4:00 a.m. in New York

it is 3:00 a.m. in Chicago

it is 1:00 a.m. in Los Angeles

AMERICAN EMBASSY

Tržiště 15

118 01 Praha 1

Czech Republic

Telephone: +420 257-022-000

Fax: +420 257-022-809

CURRENCY

Koruny

DRIVING

A gentleman drives on the right side of the road.

ELECTRICITY

230 V   50 Hz

TIPPING

Restaurants: A gentleman leaves a tip of 10%–15% of the bill.

Cabs: A gentleman leaves a tip of 10% of the fare.

Hotel: 20 koruny per bag

GENTLEMANLY PHRASES

English	*Czech*
Hello	Dobrý den
Good-bye	Na shledanou
Please	Prosim
Thank you	Děkuji
You're welcome	Prosim
Good morning	Dobré ráno
Good night	Dobrý večer
Yes	Ano
No	Ne
Excuse me	S dovolením
How are you?	Jak se máš?
I don't understand	Nerozumim
English	Anglicky

TRADITIONAL TOAST
Na zdravi

———

An informed gentleman knows that many people in Prague leave the city for the weekend to go to their country houses. This retreat to the countryside may leave the city feeling a bit empty, but it also means that the trains departing the city on Friday and returning on Sunday will be packed.

REYKJAVIK, ICELAND

It is not always wise to visit a major city on a major holiday, but New Year's Eve is the night when Reykjavik's already enviable nightlife goes into full swing, filling the air with what may well be the biggest pyrotechnic spectacle in the world. Here, especially at party time, the hardy Viking spirit survives.

DISTANCE FROM OTHER CITIES
  1,086 miles from Oslo
  1,175 miles from London
  1,389 miles from Paris
  2,611 miles from New York
  2,958 miles from Chicago
  4,313 miles from Los Angeles

AVERAGE MONTHLY TEMPERATURE

Month	Low	High
January	27	35
February	29	37
March	29	37
April	33	41
May	39	47

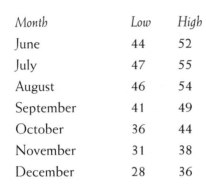

Month	Low	High
June	44	52
July	47	55
August	46	54
September	41	49
October	36	44
November	31	38
December	28	36

TIME DIFFERENCE

When it is 10:00 a.m. in Reykjavik . . .

    it is 6:00 a.m. in New York

    it is 5:00 a.m. in Chicago

    it is 4:00 a.m. in Los Angeles

AMERICAN EMBASSY

Laufásvegur 21

101 Reykjavík, Iceland

Tel: +354 562-9100

CURRENCY

Icelandic kronur

DRIVING

A gentleman drives on the right side of the road.

ELECTRICITY

220 V   50 Hz

TIPPING

There is no tipping in Iceland. The service charge is already added to most bills in restaurants.

GENTLEMANLY PHRASES

English	Icelandic
Hello	Halló
Good-bye	Bless
Please	Viltu gjöra svo vel
Thank you	Takk
You're welcome	Ekkert að þakka
Good morning	Góðan daginn
Good night	Góða nótt
Yes	Ja
No	Nei
Excuse me	Afsakið
Pleased to meet you	Komdu sæll
How are you?	Hvað segirðu gott?
Fine, thanks	Eg segi allt gott, þakka þér fyrir
I don't understand	Eg skil ekki
English	Ensku

Traditional Toast
Samtaka nu

———

An informed gentleman knows that alcohol is very expensive in Iceland and that when it is ordered with a meal it can easily double the bill. He will be wise to check the prices before ordering.

TINY TOURISTS

Traveling to a foreign country is an exciting, educational, eye-opening experience for anyone, but children who are given the opportunity to visit other countries will be gathering memories that they will treasure for the rest of their lives. When a gentleman travels with children, it is his job to make sure those memories give them—and him— sweet dreams, rather than nightmares.

Whether a gentleman is traveling with children of his own or children who belong to other people, the safety and behavior of the children in his charge are his central concern. If he is the only adult in their company, the well-being of his young companions is entirely his responsibility.

Unless the purpose of his trip is a visit to grandparents, aunts, or uncles who have never seen their recently born grandchild, niece, or nephew, a gentleman will be wise not to undertake the challenges of traveling with an infant. Not only will the trip be exhausting for the babe-in-arms, but it may also wear the gentleman's nerves and those of his fellow travelers to a frazzle. Unless he feels there is some reason he *must* take the infant with him, he will be better advised to carry along a good supply

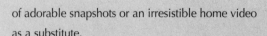

of adorable snapshots or an irresistible home video as a substitute.

In most cases, however, it is a much better idea for adult relatives to pay a visit to the *child*, if their finances and their health allow them to do so.

Even in the case of children who are slightly older, a gentleman knows that a shorter vacation is preferable to a round-the-world cruise. Children may be enchanted by the experience of a Turkish market, at least for a while, but their attention spans and their patience may give out long before the adults traveling with them are ready to head back to the hotel. Hours spent in the galleries of the Louvre will very likely leave them fidgety and foul-spirited.

A thoughtful gentleman will make sure the trip itinerary includes child-friendly activities such as a visit to an amusement park, a zoo, or a public park where children can dash across the lawns or splash in the fountains. (Children would never be allowed to play hide-and-seek in the hallways of a museum, of course.) He also makes sure they are well equipped with coloring books and crayons, video games, and other toys that will help them pass the time in a quiet and civilized way.

Even teenagers may grow weary of a constant diet of high culture. Their gentlemanly chaperon may wish to involve them in the planning of the day's activities by asking, "What would you like to do today? We could spend some time in the Victoria and Albert, and then maybe we could do some shopping."

While a gentleman may be looking forward to his trip as an adventure in exotic dining, he also knows that children, and even teenagers, often have little interest in expanding their diets. Unless they are to starve, he must at least once a day find something they will eat—even if it is something as simple as fish and chips, a gyro sandwich, or a slice of pizza. Although the best-known American fast-food restaurants have franchises in most major cities, a gentleman uses them only as a last resort and only if the children are looking pale and gaunt.

Although he does not wish to appear overly strict or overly protective, a gentleman is conscious at all times of the safety of his young companions. He does not allow them to wander out of his sight; neither does he permit them to talk to strangers, unless he is present. Even teenagers should be cautioned against roaming the streets at night, especially if they are alone.

A gentleman remembers that, before traveling abroad, even children must have a valid passport. He also makes sure they have had all necessary inoculations, and that he is aware of any allergies or other health problems they may have.

Rio de Janeiro, Brazil

Of course it's the city of Carnival (the time just before Lent), but it's a brilliant city the rest of the time as well. Off-season is much less frantic, and the Sugar Loaf cliffs consistently take the breath away.

Distance from Other Cities

219 miles from São Paulo

1,226 miles from Buenos Aires

2,812 miles from Caracas

4,825 miles from New York

5,304 miles from Chicago

6,308 miles from Los Angeles

Average Monthly Temperature

Month	Low	High
January	74	85
February	74	86
March	74	85
April	71	82
May	69	80
June	66	77
July	65	78
August	66	78

Month	Low	High
September	67	77
October	68	79
November	71	81
December	72	84

TIME DIFFERENCE

When it is 10:00 a.m. in Rio de Janeiro . . .

it is 9:00 a.m. in New York

it is 8:00 a.m. in Chicago

it is 6:00 a.m. in Los Angeles

AMERICAN CONSULATE

Av. Presidente Wilson, 147 Castelo

20030-020 - Rio de Janeiro, RJ, Brazil

Telephone: +55 21-3823-2000

Fax: +55 21-3823-2003

CURRENCY

Real

DRIVING

A gentleman drives on the right side of the road.

ELECTRICITY

110/120 V   60 Hz

Tipping

Restaurants: A service charge is traditionally added. A gentleman leaves a tip equal to 5%–10% of the bill if the service was exceptional.

Cabs: No tip is necessary.

Hotel assistance: 2 reais per bag

Gentlemanly Phrases

English	*Portuguese*
Hello	Olá
Good-bye	Adeus
Please	Por favor
Thank you	Obrigado
You're welcome	De nadah
Good morning	Bom dia
Good night	Boa noite
Yes	Sim
No	Não
Excuse me	Cum licenca
How are you?	Como está?
Fine, thanks	Bem, obrigado
I don't understand	Não compreendo
English	Inglês

TRADITIONAL TOAST
Saude!

An informed gentleman knows that when he hears South Americans talking about *futebol* (football) they are actually talking about the game known in the United States as soccer.

ROME, ITALY

Rome is the Eternal City, with the majestic ruins of the monumental Colosseum as a reminder of the grandeur of the Roman Empire. From the heights of its Seven Hills to the depths of its catacombs, Rome is a city where legend lives—wherever a gentleman turns his glance.

DISTANCE FROM OTHER CITIES
143 miles from Florence
244 miles from Venice
687 miles from Paris
4,283 miles from New York
4,816 miles from Chicago
6,339 miles from Los Angeles

AVERAGE MONTHLY TEMPERATURE

Month	Low	High
January	39	55
February	40	56
March	43	59
April	47	63
May	54	71

Month	Low	High
June	61	77
July	66	83
August	67	83
September	62	79
October	56	71
November	46	62
December	42	57

TIME DIFFERENCE

It if is 10:00 a.m. in Rome . . .

it is 4:00 a.m. in New York

it is 3:00 a.m. in Chicago

it is 1:00 a.m. in Los Angeles

AMERICAN EMBASSY

Via Vittorio Veneto 119/A

00187 Roma, Italy

Telephone:+39 06-467-41

Fax: +39 06-4882-672 or 06-4674-2356

CURRENCY

Euro

DRIVING

A gentleman drives on right side of the road.

ELECTRICITY

220 V   50Hz

TIPPING

Restaurants: A gentleman leaves a tip equal to 10% of the bill if a service charge hasn't already been added.

Cabs: A gentleman tips his driver 10% of his final fare.

Hotel assistance: Although not expected, a tip of 1 euro per bag is gladly accepted.

GENTLEMANLY PHRASES

English	*Italian*
Hello	Ciao
Good-bye	Arrivederci
Please	Per favore
Thank you	Grazie
You're welcome	Prego
Good morning	Buon giorno
Good night	Buona notte
Yes	Si
No	No

English	Italian
English	*Italian*
Excuse me	Scusi
Pleased to meet you	Molto lieto
How are you?	Come sta?
Fine, thanks	Bene, grazie
I don't understand	Non capisco
English	Inglese

TRADITIONAL TOAST

Salute

An informed gentleman knows that many retail businesses in Rome close for several hours in the afternoon. If shopping is to play a part of a gentleman's time in Rome, he plans his schedule accordingly.

SAINT PETERSBURG, RUSSIA

Once the capital city of the Russian empire, Saint
Petersburg still boasts the grandest of Mother
Russia's museums and palaces. Group excursions to
the Hermitage are available, but a gentleman may
wish to experience the richness of this palace on
his own.

DISTANCE FROM OTHER CITIES

185 miles from Helsinki

393 miles from Moscow

428 miles from Stockholm

4,280 miles from New York

4,584 miles from Chicago

5,709 miles from Los Angeles

AVERAGE MONTHLY TEMPERATURE

Month	Low	High
January	15	24
February	16	25
March	24	34
April	33	46
May	44	60
June	52	66

Month	Low	High
July	56	70
August	54	66
September	45	56
October	37	45
November	28	35
December	20	28

TIME DIFFERENCE

When it is 10:00 a.m. in Saint Petersburg . . .

it is 2:00 a.m. in New York

it is 1:00 a.m. in Chicago

it is 11 p.m. in Los Angeles

AMERICAN EMBASSY

Ulitsa Furshtatskaya, 15

St. Petersburg 191028, Russia

Telephone: +7 812-331-2600

Fax: +7 812-331-2852

CURRENCY

Ruble

DRIVING

A gentleman drives on the right side of the road.

ELECTRICITY

220 V 50 Hz

TIPPING

Restaurants: A gentleman leaves a tip equal to 10% of the bill, unless a service charge has already been added.

Cabs: A gentleman tips his driver 10% of his final fare.

Hotel: 25 rubles per bag

GENTLEMANLY PHRASES

English	Russian
Hello	Priviet
Good-bye	Da svi`daniya
Please	Pa`zhalsta
Thank you	Spa`siba
You're welcome	Pa`zhalsta
Good morning	Dobroye utro
Good night	Dobroye noch
Yes	Dah
No	Nyet
Excuse me	Izvi`neete
Pleased to meet you	Priyatno s vami poznakomitsa

English	*Russian*
How are you?	Kak de`la?
Fine, thanks	Ya, spa`siba
I don't understand	Ya ne pani`mayu
English	Awngleeski

TRADITIONAL TOAST
  Za nas

Unless he speaks fluent Russian, an informed gentleman makes arrangements in advance with his hotel or travel agent for transportation from the airport to his hotel.

Airborne

Once a gentleman's flight has left the ground, he remains a customer of the airline and can expect courteous, efficient service from its employees. But he also has become, for the coming hours, a member of a small community, a community that has its own rules and its own codes of behavior.

It does not matter whether a gentleman is flying first class, business class, or coach. He does his best to comply with the requests and instructions of the flight attendants in order to help guarantee a pleasant and safe flight for himself and his fellow passengers. He turns off his electronic equipment even before he is asked to do so, and he remains quiet and attentive while the flight attendants explain the procedures to be followed in case of an emergency. He will be wise to make a last-minute visit to the restroom, since, especially on some flights departing from major U.S. cities, passengers may be required to remain in their seats for the first 30 minutes of the flight.

If carry-on bags are permitted on his flight, a gentleman makes sure they fit easily into the overhead bins in the cabin. He does his best not to force the line of passengers behind him to back up while he struggles with an oversize bag. If he realizes that he is indeed blocking the aisle, he simply says, "I'm sorry," to the people behind him. If he realizes that his bag is unlikely to fit in the bin, he sets it temporarily in his seat, steps out of the aisle, and waits until a flight attendant is available to assist him.

If a gentleman notices that a fellow passenger is having difficulty stowing his or her bag, and if he is tall enough and agile enough to be of real assistance, he offers a hand to help push the bag into the bin. He does not demean a fellow passenger by muttering, "Hey, why don't you move it, sister?" or "What's the matter? Do you think you're the only person on this plane?"

Once his flight has left the airport, a gentleman remains in his seat, with his seat belt fastened, unless he must make a trip to the restroom. Unless he has a circulatory problem that makes it risky for him to remain seated for extended periods of time, he does not roam up and down the aisles, chatting with friends and obstructing the path of the flight attendants and the beverage cart.

On a flight of any duration, a gentleman does not attempt to force his fellow passengers to engage in conversation with him. A cordial "Hello, how are you?" is all he really needs to offer. If the fellow passenger seems interested in pursuing a conversation, he may proceed to make pleasant small talk. In no case does he allow the conversation to grow so loud as to intrude on the privacy of others passengers. If he has brought along his iPod or other personal entertainment system, he keeps the volume turned to a reasonable level, knowing that, although he may be wearing his ear buds, the sound can still disturb the peace of his fellow flyers.

Although a gentleman may find it difficult to sleep during any flight, he realizes that others may wish to get as much rest as possible during the course of the trip. He remains quiet and does his best to stay within the confines of his seat. If he wishes to read, he keeps his reading light turned to the lowest level he finds usable. He does not attempt to soothe his restlessness by too frequent purchases from the beverage cart.

As the flight nears its destination, he once again follows the directions of the flight attendants. He does not leap up from his seat or start yammering into his cell phone the second the plane has

landed. Instead, he takes his place in line along
with the other passengers, pulling his carry-on bag
from the bin as swiftly and as carefully as possible.
He does not want to hold up the line, but neither
does he want to risk causing the passenger behind
him to suffer a concussion.

In all cases, while he is on a plane, just as when
he in an airport, a gentleman understands that all
passengers are expected to abide by the safety rules
and restrictions. He knows that they are not
directed specifically at him. On the other hand, if
he notices that another passenger is involved in
what may be risky behavior or that another passenger seems to be in distress, he alerts a flight attendant as soon as possible.

SEOUL, SOUTH KOREA

Autumn is the perfect season for a visit to Seoul. On a clear fall day, from atop Namsan, the mountain in the middle of the city, the panorama of the fifth largest city in the world spreads before you. Much of Seoul was rebuilt in the wake of the Korean War, but ancient temples and a culture of quiet dignity still survive.

DISTANCE FROM OTHER CITIES

    141 miles from Pusan

    550 miles from Shanghai

    719 miles from Tokyo

    5,960 miles from Los Angeles

    6,536 miles from Chicago

    6,872 miles from New York

AVERAGE MONTHLY TEMPERATURE

Month	Low	High
January	21	33
February	25	38
March	35	49
April	46	62
May	55	72

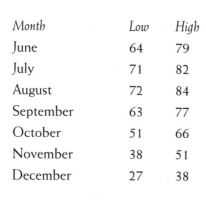

Month	Low	High
June	64	79
July	71	82
August	72	84
September	63	77
October	51	66
November	38	51
December	27	38

TIME DIFFERENCE

When it is 10:00 a.m. in Seoul . . .

it is 9:00 p.m. the previous day in New York

it is 8:00 p.m. the previous day in Chicago

it is 6:00 p.m. the previous day in Los Angeles

AMERICAN EMBASSY

32 Sejongno, Jongno-gu
Seoul 110-710
Republic of Korea
Telephone: +82 2-397-4114

CURRENCY

Won

Driving

A gentleman drives on the right side of the road.

Electricity

220 V   60 Hz

Tipping

Restaurants: No tip is necessary.

Cabs: No tip is necessary.

Hotel assistance: 100 won per bag

Gentlemanly Phrases

English	Korean
Hello	Annyoung
Good-bye	Annyoungi gaseyo
Please	But'ak hamnida
Thank you	Kamsa hamnida
You're welcome	Cheon maneyo
Good morning	Joh-eun ah-chim-imnida
Good night	Joh-eun bamimnida
Yes	Ye
No	Anio
Excuse me	Juay song hamnida
Pleased to meet you	Mannaseo pangapseumnida
How are you?	Eo-ddeo'ke ji naeshimnikka?
Fine, thanks	Jal jinaemnida

English	Korean
I don't understand	Ee-haega ankamnida
English	Yong eo-reul

TRADITIONAL TOAST
Gung bai

An informed gentleman knows Korean names usually consist of at least three words and the surname is given first during introductions.

STOCKHOLM, SWEDEN

The sun is low during some months, but it rides
high in the sky almost all day at other times of the
year. It is even possible, at the height of summer,
to get a burn at the beach. All year round,
however, bronze sculptures of blithesome dancers
cavort through the public fountains, no matter
what the time of day or the temperature.

DISTANCE FROM OTHER CITIES
   246 miles from Helsinki
   258 miles from Oslo
   428 miles from Saint Petersburg
   3,927 miles from New York
   4,280 miles from Chicago
   5,524 miles from Los Angeles

AVERAGE MONTHLY TEMPERATURE

Month	Low	High
January	22	30
February	22	30
March	27	37
April	34	47
May	43	60

Month	Low	High
June	52	69
July	56	71
August	54	68
September	48	59
October	41	49
November	33	40
December	26	34

TIME DIFFERENCE

When it is 10:00 a.m. in Stockholm . . .

it is 4:00 a.m. in New York

it is 3:00 a.m. in Chicago

it is 1:00 a.m. in Los Angeles

AMERICAN EMBASSY

Dag Hammarskjölds Väg 31

SE-115 89 Stockholm, Sweden

Telephone: +46 8-783-5300

CURRENCY

Krona

DRIVING

A gentleman drives on the right side of the road.

Electricity

230 V   50 Hz

Tipping

Restaurants: A gentleman leaves a tip equal to 5%–10% of his bill for excellent service, in addition to the service charge.

Cabs: A gentleman gives his driver a tip by rounding up the fare to the nearest kronor.

Hotel assistance: A gentleman may use his discretion, but 5 kronor per bag is acceptable.

Gentlemanly Phrases

English	*Swedish*
Hello	Hej
Good-bye	Hej da
Please	Snälla
Thank you	Tack
You're welcome	Varsågod
Good morning	God morgon
Good night	God natt
Yes	Ja
No	Nej
Excuse me	Ursäkta
How are you?	Hur mär du?

English	*Swedish*
Fine, thanks	Jag mär bra, tack
I don't understand	Jag förstår inte
English	Engelska

TRADITIONAL TOAST
Skal

An informed gentleman knows that when he goes to the cash register in Sweden, he is expected to place his purchases on the counter with the barcode turned upward and toward the cashier. This small courtesy has become a tradition in this city of courteous people.

Sydney, Australia

The Sydney Opera House seems to fly out over the harbor, and the beaches glisten in the sunshine, provided you're there in the middle of winter—which is actually summer, Down Under. And yes, Australians will greet you with a jolly "G'day, mate." And they'll mean it.

Distance from Other Cities
443 miles from Melbourne

454 miles from Brisbane

1,340 miles from Auckland

7,508 miles from Los Angeles

9,251 miles from Chicago

9,946 miles from New York

Average Monthly Temperature

Month	Low	High
January	65	79
February	65	79
March	63	77
April	57	73
May	51	68
June	46	63

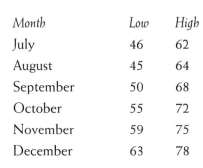

Month	Low	High
July	46	62
August	45	64
September	50	68
October	55	72
November	59	75
December	63	78

TIME DIFFERENCE

When it is 10:00 a.m. in Sydney . . .

it is 8:00 p.m. the previous day in New York

it is 7:00 p.m. in Chicago

it is 5:00 p.m. in Los Angeles

AMERICAN CONSULATE

MLC Centre
Level 10
19-29 Martin Place
Sydney NSW 2000, Australia
Telephone: +61 2-9373-9200

CURRENCY

Australian dollar

DRIVING

A gentleman drives on the left side of the road.

ELECTRICITY

240 V   50 Hz

TIPPING

Restaurants: Tipping is not expected in Australian restaurants. However, if a gentleman has received exceptional service, he may wish to tip his server 10% of the bill.

Cabs: A gentleman does not tip the driver, unless the service has been above and beyond the call of duty.

Hotels: 1 Australian dollar per bag

AUSTRALIAN PHRASES

Australian	American
Aussie	Australian
Bloke	Man
Bottle shop	Liquor shop
G'day	Hello
Hire	To rent (as in "to hire a car")
Mate	Friend
Oz	Australia
Sheila	Woman

TRADITIONAL TOAST
Cheers

———

An informed gentleman knows that Australian sunlight has very high UV levels and skin damage can occur quickly, especially during the middle of the day. A gentleman keeps sunscreen handy to prevent burns and sun damage.

TOKYO, JAPAN

Tokyo is a big city with a bustling nightlife, but its
traditional glories, such as the quiet ritual of the
tea ceremony or a sky full of cherry blossoms, can
offer the most delicate enchantments. Amidst
these pleasures, a gentleman will still remember to
remove his shoes before stepping into even the
busiest sushi bar.

DISTANCE FROM OTHER CITIES
    251 miles from Osaka
    515 miles from Sapporo
    719 miles from Seoul
    6,744 miles from New York
    6,302 miles from Chicago
    5,478 miles from Los Angeles

AVERAGE MONTHLY TEMPERATURE

Month	Low	High
January	34	49
February	35	49
March	39	54
April	50	64
May	58	73

Month	Low	High
June	65	77
July	72	83
August	75	87
September	68	80
October	57	70
November	48	61
December	39	53

Time Difference

When it is 10:00 a.m. in Tokyo . . .

it is 9:00 p.m. the previous day in New York

it is 8:00 p.m. the previous day in Chicago

it is 6:00 p.m. the previous day in Los Angeles

American Embassy

1-10-5 Akasaka, Minato-ku

Tokyo 107-8420, Japan

Telephone: +81 03-3224-5000

Currency

Yen

Driving

A gentleman drives on the left side of the road.

Electricity

100 V   50 Hz

Tipping

It is not customary to tip in Japan.

Gentlemanly Phrases

English	Japanese
Hello	Konnichiwa
Good-bye	Sayonara
Please	Kudasai
Thank you	Arogato
You're welcome	Do itashimashite
Good morning	Ohayo gozaimasu
Good night	Oyasumi nasai
Yes	Hai
No	Iie
Excuse me	Sumimasen
How are you?	Ogenki desu ka?
Fine, thanks	Hai, genki desu
I don't understand	Watashi wa wakarimasen

TRADITIONAL TOAST
Omedeto gozaimasu

————

An informed gentleman knows that bowing is still the customary greeting in Japan. Although a handshake is common in business situations involving Westerners, a slight bow from the waist is still customary.

Group Dynamics

For many a gentleman, a trip abroad is an entirely personal matter—the culmination of a lifelong dream to see certain sights and experience certain local customs and traditions. Accordingly, a gentleman may wish to follow his own itinerary, one that caters to his interests and desires.

On the other hand, a gentleman may also be attracted by the idea of traveling in a group. That group may consist of a close-knit coterie of friends and/or family members. Or it may be a group organized by the gentleman's office (perhaps as a reward for superior performance on the job), by his church or synagogue, or by some civic organization of which he is a member. It may even be a group put together by a travel agency, university, museum, or historical society, with the goal of bringing together a group of people who share common interests, even if they have never met one another before.

In all cases, whenever he is traveling with a group, a gentleman hopes to find himself in the company of like-minded, amicable travelers. At least that is his hope when he agrees to traveling in the company of others. At its best, group travel led by a knowledgeable, professional guide can be a dream come true, with every major activity organized, and many expenses paid ahead of time. A tour group may also end up having access to special events and restricted sites, which the gentleman might find difficult to arrange on his own.

Because human beings are simply human, however, a gentleman may find himself trapped with a group of fellow tourists whom he does not find at all congenial. At that point, it is his responsibility to make the best of the situation, do what he can to have the best time possible, and try his best not to exacerbate the awkwardness of his condition—or the condition of others in his tour group.

Before signing up for a group tour, a gentleman makes sure to read all brochures provided by the sponsoring agency or organization. He visits its Web site and makes sure he is confident in his decision before sending in his deposit money.

Nevertheless, hardly any trip can be guaranteed to turn out precisely the way the gentleman envisioned it. Once he is on foreign soil, unless he feels threatened in terms of safety or in terms of his health, there will be no use in his complaining to anyone, except to the leader of the tour. Even then, there may be little the tour leader can do, except perhaps to move the gentleman to a more pleasant hotel room or help him find a roommate who does not snore quite so loudly.

What's more, the gentleman may discover that the itinerary for the trip is not what he expected it to be, or he may not approve the choice of restaurants. If such turns out to be the case, it is his responsibility to have as good a time as he possibly can. He may wish to move to a hotel that is more to his liking, arrange his daytime activities on his own, or make his own dinner reservations.

If he makes those choices, however, a gentleman understands that he is doing so at his own expense. He respectfully informs the group leader of his plans and keeps a record of the extra expenses he has incurred. (However, unless he has incurred these expenses because he fears for his own health or his own safety, he will have little chance of being reimbursed for the extra dollars that he has spent, even if he is convinced he has not received full value for his money.) It must be his personal decision whether he toughs it out and stays with the group, or heads out on his own, in hopes of a happier experience.

If he is traveling with family members or with friends, a gentleman may feel he has no such option. Even in those cases, he is always his own man, and he makes that fact clear from the very first discussion of the trip. He may wish to visit sites that other friends do not wish to visit. He may wish to rest in the afternoon or sleep in late in the morning. He simply says, "I know you want to visit the gardens. Why don't you do that? I'll do the art museum this afternoon, and we can meet back at the hotel at six." That way, nobody gets bored, and the gentleman's friends may end up being so excited about the gardens that he will decide to put them on his own agenda for the next day.

Unfortunately, whether he is traveling with people he knows, people whom he hardly knows at all, or people whom he has never met, a gentleman sometimes discovers that he is traveling in the company of a boor or a bore. To make matters worse, the boorish or boring person may feel it is his responsibility to organize activities for the entire group, saying, "We'll start tomorrow at seven at the cathedral; then we can tour the pyramids at ten, and I understand there's a cappuccino bar where we can have lunch right after that, and we can probably work in the gondola ride and a visit to the panda house at the pagoda before sunset."

Even worse is the fellow traveler who can hardly be satisfied with anything. He quickly loses interest with "all those museums" or "all those mountains and all that snow." The food in the restaurants is "too spicy" or "too pricey."

In all these cases, a gentleman sticks to his guns, has the best time he possibly can, and says, "I'll meet you back at the hotel at six."

VIENNA, AUSTRIA

There's a homey, sentimental feel to the City of Dreams. Coffee houses, the progenitors of Starbucks, are in abundance, and people still gather there to sip and chat. Some of the greatest movements of twentieth-century art, such as the Wiener Werkstätte, were born here—in the city that also gave birth to the waltz.

DISTANCE FROM OTHER CITIES
    156 miles from Salzburg
    156 miles from Prague
    239 miles from Munich
    4,225 miles from New York
    4,692 miles from Chicago
    6,109 miles from Los Angeles

AVERAGE MONTHLY TEMPERATURE

Month	Low	High
January	27	36
February	28	39
March	35	49
April	41	57
May	49	67

Month	Low	High
June	55	72
July	59	77
August	55	77
September	53	69
October	43	57
November	35	44
December	30	37

TIME DIFFERENCE

When it is 10:00 a.m. in Vienna . . .

it is 4:00 a.m. in New York

it is 3:00 a.m. in Chicago

it is 1:00 a.m. in Los Angeles

AMERICAN EMBASSY

Boltzmanngasse 16

A-1090 Vienna, Austria

Telephone: +43 1-31339-0

Fax: +43 1-310-06-82

CURRENCY

Euro

DRIVING

A gentleman drives on the right side of the road.

Electricity

230 V   50 Hz

Tipping

Restaurants: A gentleman leaves a tip equal to 10% of the bill.

Cabs: A gentleman tips his driver 10% of the fare.

Hotel assistance: 1 euro per bag

Gentlemanly Phrases

English	*German*
Hello	Guten Tag
Good-bye	Auf Wiedersehen
Please	Bitte
Thank you	Danke
You're welcome	Bitte schön
Good morning	Guten Morgen
Good night	Gute Nacht
Yes	Ja
No	Nein
Excuse me	Entschuldigen Sie
Pleased to meet you	Sie kennenzulernen
How are you?	Wie geht es Ihnen?
Fine, thanks	Gut, danke

English	German
I don't understand	Ich verstehe nicht
English	Englisch

TRADITIONAL TOAST
Prosit

An informed gentleman knows that he must stop by the nearest gas station to purchase a *vignette*, his ticket to the Austrian roadways.

ZURICH, SWITZERLAND

The elegant spires of medieval churches reach
up into the air, but Zurich's cobbled streets
lead to museums filled with some of the
greatest modern art collections in the world.
The history of the city is romantic, but it is
also the banking center of the world. Expect to
see briefcases.

DISTANCE FROM OTHER CITIES

59 miles from Bern

138 miles from Geneva

304 miles from Paris

3,931 miles from New York

4,435 miles from Chicago

5,925 miles from Los Angeles

AVERAGE MONTHLY TEMPERATURE

Month	Low	High
January	27	37
February	28	40
March	34	49
April	38	55
May	46	65

Month	Low	High
June	52	70
July	56	75
August	55	74
September	50	68
October	43	56
November	34	45
December	30	39

TIME DIFFERENCE

When it is 10:00 a.m. in Zurich . . .

it is 4:00 a.m. in New York

it is 3:00 a.m. in Chicago

it is 1:00 a.m. in Los Angeles

AMERICAN CONSULATE

Dufourstrasse 101

3rd floor

Zurich, Switzerland

Mailing Address:

Dufourstrasse 101

CH-8008 Zurich, Switzerland

Telephone: +41 1-422-25-66

Fax: +41 1-499-29-61

CURRENCY

Swiss franc

DRIVING

A gentleman drives on the right side of the road.

ELECTRICITY

230 V   50 Hz

TIPPING

Restaurants: A gentleman leaves a tip equal to 10% of the bill, unless a service charge has already been included.

Cabs: A gentleman tips his driver 10% of the fare.

Hotel assistance: 1 euro per bag

GENTLEMANLY PHRASES

In French

English	French
Hello	Bonjour
Good-bye	Au revoir
Please	S'il vous plaît
Thank you	Merci
You're welcome	De rien
Good morning	Bonjour

English	French
Good night	Bonne nuit
Yes	Oui
No	Non
Excuse me	Pardonnez-moi
Pleased to meet you	Enchanté
How are you?	Comment allez-vous?
Fine, thanks	Bien, merci
I don't understand	Je ne comprends pas
English	Anglais

In German

English	German
Hello	Guten Tag
Good-bye	Auf Wiedersehen
Please	Bitte
Thank you	Danke
You're welcome	Bitte schön
Good morning	Guten Morgen
Good night	Gute Nacht
Yes	Ja
No	Nein
Excuse me	Entschuldigen Sie
Pleased to meet you	Sie kennenzulernen
How are you?	Wie geht es Ihnen?

English	German
English	*German*
Fine, thanks	Gut, danke
I don't understand	Ich verstehe nicht
English	Englisch

TRADITIONAL TOAST

A votre santé

Although German may be the language most often heard in Zurich, French and Italian are also common. An informed gentleman acquaints himself with the most frequently used phrases in all three languages.